TACTICAL
ANTHROPOLOGY

To Megan, Julia, and Daniel
for being our greatest joys in life
and
to our federal, state and local friends in emergency
response, law enforcement, disaster relief, and the
military for their tireless efforts to make our
communities safer every day.

We would also like to express their deepest gratitude to
Alli Jason for her editorial assistance.

TACTICAL ANTHROPOLOGY

A Practical Guide for Emergency and Disaster Response in Culturally Complex Communities

by
Mark A. Grey, Ph.D.
and
Michele K. Devlin, Dr.P.H.

Published by
Mission Forward Media

Cover photo credits: Top left: FEMA photo by Ryan Courtade. Top right: FEMA. Bottom left: FEMA Photo by Michael Rieger. Bottom Right: Photo by Michele Devlin. Back cover credits: Left: FEMA photo by Samir Valeja. Center; FEMA photo by Brittany Trotter. Right: FEMA Photo by George Armstrong.

TACTICAL ANTHROPOOGY
TABLE OF CONTENTS

SECTION IV: RESOURCES AND TOOLS

PREFACE:

THE GROWING NEED FOR TACTICAL ANTHROPOLOGY

The Growing Need for Tactical Anthropology

New patterns in globalization, economic connections, migration, conflict, and human displacement have contributed to the rapid diversification of numerous communities throughout the United States and other areas of the world. Dramatic population shifts are occurring both in large urban areas and in rural communities.

Micro-plurality, or the intense diversification of culturally complex communities, presents unique challenges and opportunities for public safety and emergency response organizations during disasters and humanitarian crises. Too often, residents such as immigrants, refugees, ethnic minorities, low-income families, and other vulnerable populations are disproportionately affected by disasters and emergencies.

Many public safety organizations have little or no contact or experience with these at-risk populations and are sometimes even unaware of their presence in their areas of operation. Public safety professionals typically have little understanding of the cultural, linguistic, financial, and related barriers these populations can face during emergencies and disasters. They often struggle to provide services to these communities in an effective manner, and can be frustrated when when their well-meaning efforts fail, particularly during disasters and large scale emergencies.

Public safety agencies increasingly need to develop cross-cultural tactics, techniques, and procedures that can help them better meet the needs of marginalized populations within their jurisdictions with times of crisis. The development of a tactical anthropology skill set and the creation of Cultural Asset Teams within public safety agencies can provide urgently needed expertise in a variety of areas for these at-risk communities.

Public safety, emergency medical, fire, disaster planners, and other first responders will find this book "Tactical Anthropology" to be an easy-to-use, valuable resource for working effectively in complex, chaotic, and uncertain situations with populations from multiple cultural backgrounds. This practical guide is designed for working professionals and students in a variety of first responder fields, including public safety, fire, emergency medical services (EMS), disaster relief, emergency management, local government, public health, and other occupations. This text provides a step-by-step introduction to why populations around the world are changing so quickly, outlines the implications of these changes for first responders, and provides practical strategies to work cross-culturally in rapidly changing environments.

Tactical Anthropology can also be used as a classroom guide for trainers in first responder fields. Section I provides narrative overview, in simple to understand terms, about how communities are changing around the world and how first responders must understand these cultural changes to protect civilians, minimize risk to themselves, and address threats such as disasters and large scale emergencies. Section II provides an in-depth discussion of how Tactical Anthropology skills are urgently needed in a variety of occupational fields during emergency response, and how these cultural assets can be utilized effectively. Each chapter in Section III is designed to be a one-hour training or briefing for first responders. These chapters provide concise information on the main cross-cultural tactics, techniques, and procedures needed by emergency responders working in multicultural environments before, during, and after crisis situations. Scenarios and drills are also included after each of these chapters for classroom exercises. Section IV provides resources, lists, and other tools that can be used quickly when working in the Tactical Anthropology field.

Tactical Anthropology helps fill the knowledge and skills gap seen too often in today's emergency response and public safety fields, and can help professionals and students ensure the safety and well-being of all populations within rapidly diversifying and culturally complex areas of operation in times of crisis.

SECTION I:

AN INTRODUCTION TO TACTICAL ANTHROPOLOGY

1. TODAY'S RAPIDLY CHANGING COMMUNITIES

Bottom Line Up Front (BLUF):

• The world's population is growing faster, mostly in developing countries.

• The world's population is more mobile than ever and most movement will be from poor countries to richer countries.

• Most humans live in cities now and increasingly in communities that are particularly prone to disasters and large scale emergencies.

• Cultural diversity has become so complex today in many communities that government categories on race and ethnicity are no longer meaningful for many agencies involved in emergency management and disaster planning.

Photo 1.1 A parade of survivors commemorate the tenth anniversary of Hurricane Katrina in New Orleans, August 2015. (Photo by Samuel Carr McKay/FEMA photo.)

For most of us, a community is a place we share with other people with whom we interact in the normal course of our lives like our neighbors, our co-workers and the children who attend school with our children. We are not all friends and there may be many differences among us in terms of lifestyles, politics and status, but we generally draw around us a circle that makes our community different from others. In the classic sense, a community is defined by what its members have in common, but also by what it does not have in common with other people and places in the nation or world. Although it is common to move among communities in one's lifetime, humans still tend to develop concepts of "us" versus "them." Despite that fact that with new Internet and smart phone technology we hold access to knowledge about the the world in our hands, we still tend to believe that what happens in other communities, cultures, and nations has no impact on "us" or our community.

However, the early decades of the 21st century are proving us wrong. Global events do have local consequences. For many people we serve in the emergency response field, realizing how population and cultural changes in other regions of the world can impact our own local communities is challenging and difficult. This is especially true among our colleagues in law enforcement, emergency management, and disaster relief, and emergency medical services. Their jobs are already stressful enough not knowing where the next call may take them or how their actions may endanger themselves or others. But now we lay on top of these day-to-day concerns how their communities, jurisdictions, and service areas are becoming more culturally, linguistically, and ethnically diverse and how challenges that used to be faced in "other" towns and regions of the world are now appearing in their communities. Before going into the many implications of global population change for first responders, it will be helpful to first and briefly review some of the key global trends that increasingly manifest themselves in local communities around the world.

1. The world's total population in 2017 was about 7 billion. It is expected to continue growing. Middle-range projections by the United Nations Population Fund suggest the world's population will grow to ten billion by about 2050 and about eleven billion at the end of the 21st century. Higher and lower projections for the end of the 21st century are 16.5 billion and 7 billion respectively, depending on trends in fertility rates, which in general are projected to decline.

2. Most of the world's population growth will take place in less developed regions of the world. The fastest growing populations are in Africa and the Middle East, with slower but significant population growth in Asia and Latin America. Populations are actually shrinking in many Eastern European nations, Russia, and Japan.

3. The world's population is also getting younger. In 2016, about 1.8 billion people in the world were between the ages of 10 and 24. Young people make up the majority of populations in the world's 48 less developed countries. Their future prospects will depend on investments in education, job opportunities and access to information.

4. For decades, the general flow of economic migrants has been from low-income nations in the "Global South" towards wealthier nations in the "Global North," like the United States, France, the United Kingdom and Germany. Between 1950 and 2015, Europe, North America and Oceania have been net *receivers* of international migration. Africa, Asia, Latin America and the Caribbean have been net *exporters* of migrants. Between 2000 and 2015, the world's high-income nations like the United States and Germany received an average of 4.1 million net migrants annually. Larger numbers of migrants are expected from poor nations to middle-income developing nations like Brazil in the Global South. Income disparities between low- or middle-income nations and the world's wealthier nations will continue to drive most economic migration. Indeed, between 2015 and 2050, the top net receivers of international migration will be the United States, Canada, the United Kingdom, Australia, Germany, the Russian Federation and Italy.

5. Net international migration will provide badly needed population in nations like the United States and the United Kingdom as birth rates in high-income nations will continue to decline and populations age. For some high-income countries, net migration may account for as much as 82 percent of population growth between 2015 and 2050.

6. Most humans now live in cities. Urbanization refers to the process through which nations and regions see the proportion of people living in rural areas decline while the proportion of people living cities, suburbs and "peri-urban" settlements ("slums") grows. Urbanization has been underway for thousands of years, but it accelerated in recent years. The United Nations estimated that 2007 was the first year that more than half of human beings in urban areas. By 2050, about 66 percent of the world's population will live in cities with most living in urban environments. In the United States and other developed nations, urbanization has been underway for over a century, and many regions in these nations already find the majority of their populations residing in cities and suburbs.

7. Forced migration is growing. Forced migration is due to increased numbers of people leaving their home communities to avoid war, ethnic conflict, genocide, and other reasons that would make people fear death or persecution. Today, we have seen more people forcibly displaced from their home communities at any time since World War II. Indeed, the United Nations High Commissioner for Refugees (UNHCR) estimates that 65.3 million people in the world have been displaced. Most, about 44 million, were displaced from their homes but remained in their nations of origin. Because they cross international borders, refugees around the world garner more media attention. However, Internally Displaced Persons (IDPs) that cannot escape from their own nations actually outnumber refugees by a ratio of almost two-to-one. The UNHCR estimates the world's refugee population at 21.3 million, with more than half under 18 years of age. In addition, there are some 10 million "stateless" people in the world with no nationality or rights to basic needs such as health care, employment, freedom of movement and education. As result of conflict or persecution, about 34,000 people around the world are forcibly displaced on a daily basis.

8. The number of "environmental" or "climate change" refugees is growing around the world. Warming sea waters are contributing to major changes in climate patterns, and severe weather events are displacing people in growing numbers. The cause of climate change and severe weather events is often a hotly debated topic in American politics, but the International Organization for Migration (IOM) states that "gradual and sudden environmental changes are already resulting in substantial population movements. The number of storms, droughts and floods has increased threefold over the last 30 years, with devastating effects on vulnerable communities, particularly in the developing world." Already millions of people have become "climate change refugees" or "environmental refugees" and their numbers are expected to grow. Forecasts for the number of environmental refugees between now and 2050 range from 25 million to 1 billion, although the IOM suggests the figure most commonly projected is 200 million. The major question is, where are these environmental refugees going? "In their desperation, these people feel they have no alternative but to seek sanctuary elsewhere…all have abandoned their homelands on a semi-permanent if not permanent basis, with little hope of a foreseeable return." It was recognized as early as 1995 that one critical challenge for people displaced by climate change is the reluctance of governments and international agencies to even recognize the environmental refugee problem and/or to even determine an appropriate label for these migrants, a problem we share in public safety and emergency management agencies across the globe.

Of course, international migration does not account for all demographics shifts. Populations change and move within nations as well. In the United States and other developed, western nations, the majority of people are white and of European descent. But this "majority" population is aging. Due to lower fertility rates, white people will not keep their majority status beyond the next two or three generations. Other "non-white" populations are growing faster with higher fertility rates and immigration. At some point in the not-so-distant future, all of the "minority" populations in the United States and other nations will outnumber the former "majority" white population. It has already occurred in a handful of American states including California. The awkward phrase that is often used to describe this situation is "majority-minority." We prefer to think of this demographic shift as an "Anglo Inversion."

When nations like the United States use legal categories to count residents and assign them a race and/or ethnicity, broad categories like those used in the U.S. Census are social categories imposed on people. They cannot reflect the tremendous cultural and ethnic diversity within Census categories. A "white" person could be from North Africa, Eastern Europe or Canada and speak any of hundreds of languages. A "black" person can be an African-American descendant of slaves brought to the New World hundreds of years ago, or an African refugee, or a French-speaking immigrant from Haiti. The growing ethnic, religious, and linguistic diversity found in many western nations and across the globe is now found in almost every community large and small.

In addition to ethnic and linguistic diversification, internal migration is on the rise. In most cases, internal migration in the developed world has to do with economic shifts and the availability of jobs. In fewer cases, we have de facto Internally Displaced People (IDPs) forced to leave their home communities because of natural and technical disasters. The thousands of people displaced within the U.S. after Hurricane Katrina provide a prime example. In the United States, people leave dangerous neighborhoods in large cities like Chicago and seek safer communities, housing, and quality schools for their children.

The global and national trends outlined above help us understand the size and movement of the world's population. We must also understand that within these larger populations there is tremendous diversity in terms of cultures, languages, religions, race and ethnicity, expectations and social practices. Among the world's growing and increasingly mobile populations, we must recognize the hundreds of ways that people differentiate themselves in terms of forming identities as members of one culture and--just as important-- how they differ from, and are not members of, other groups. People do not stop being who they are when they cross a state or national border. People bring to their new nations and communities their cultural practices, attitudes, and beliefs. They remain loyal to their faiths. They don't automatically give up their native languages and speak only the language of their new communities. They cling to their identities and continue to organize themselves as they did back home.

We are witnessing across the world what we call "rapid ethnic diversification." This describes how many communities have gone from experiencing only one or a handful of cultures and languages to experiencing many new languages, cultures and faiths. As the number of these newcomers grow, communities experience what we call "micro-plurality" or "micro-diversity" or the growing presence of many new, unique cultures and ethnicities in smaller, even rural, environments. In larger mega-urban communities, our European colleagues call this phenomenon "super diversity." These growing trends of micro-diversity and rapid ethnic diversification are creating significant challenges for emergency responders around the world, as their areas of operation become increasingly more culturally complex than ever before.

Further Reading

- Mike Davis (2007). *Planet of Slums*. New York: Verso.
- Christian Parenti (2011). *Tropic of Chaos: Climate Change and the New Geography of Violence*. New York: Nation Books.
- David Kilcullen (2013). *Out of the Mountains: The Coming Age of the Urban Guerilla*. Oxford University Press.

References

- *United Nations Social and Economic Affairs/Population Division*, World Population Prospects, 2015 Revision.
- Mike Davis (2006) *Planet of Slums,* New York: Verso.
United Nations High Commissioner for Refugees, Global Trends 2015.
- International Organization for Migration, *Migration, Climate Change and the Environment*, 2015.
- Noman Myers and J. Kent (1995). *Environmental Exodus: An Emergent Crisis in the Global Arena.* The Climate Institute, Washington, D.C. and Norman Myers (2001). Environmental Refugees: Our Latest Understanding, Philosophical Transactions of the Royal Society B:356: 16.1-16.5.:
- Norman Myers (2005). *Environmental Refugees: An Emergent Security Issue,* 13th Economic Forum, Prague, 23-17 May 2005.

2. THE IMPLICATIONS OF CULTURAL CHANGE FOR FIRST RESPONDERS

Bottom Line Up Front (BLUF):

• Human culture can be thought of as a complex set of beliefs, attitudes, and practices commonly held by a group of people that guides them on how they should expect to function together in their society. It is like the instruction manual for a group of people about how they should behave together.

• Culture is far more complex than just what food people eat, what holidays they celebrate, or what traditional clothes they wear.

• Cultural experiences generate expectations for how to act in emergencies that may differ from the expectations of public safety professionals responding to those emergencies.

Photo 2.1 Urban Search and Rescue (USAR) teams search for survivors of Hurricane Matthew in Lumberton, North Carolina, October 20116. (Photo by Jocelyn Augustino/FEMA Photo.)

Cultural, ethnic, and linguistic diversification in communities presents a number of challenges and opportunities for law enforcement, first responders, and emergency management personnel in emergency and disaster settings. Before we outline some of the critical issues in multicultural communities, let's define culture.

Anthropology is the study of human culture. The vast majority of people served by first responders are not anthropologists and thinking about human culture--much less defining it--is just not something they do. But the fact that most people don't think about their culture means that it is working. In other words, exactly because most of us don't give a second thought to how we live our day-to-day lives, or share the rules for life or hold common norms and values, means that our culture works for us. One analogy we use is that people don't realize they live in culture, the same way fish don't realize they live in water. In groups of people that are culturally similar or homogenous, everyone seems to be using the same "play book" or cultural instruction manual about how to behave and interact with each other. It's only after we are taken outside the comfort zone of our culture that we start to realize how it works for us.

We humans are not only the products of our culture, but throughout our lifetimes we also recreate and regenerate our shared culture. Human culture provides guidance for how we live our lives, how we raise children, how we interact with others, and even how we respond to people in authority. When most people are asked to talk about other cultures, they point to obvious cultural traits and practices like fashion, language, holidays, food, and art. But these visible cultural symbols often hide the deeper elements of culture that present the greatest challenges to understanding and working with diverse populations.

Deeper culture, which can take years to grasp in some cases, includes things like taboos, rituals, values, gender expectations, manners, authority, courtship and marriage, social class, time orientation, and so forth. Culture gives guidance about some of life's trickier questions like, "Who is acceptable for my son or daughter to marry?" "What are our obligations to parents?" or "How do we show respect to people with a lower status in society?" Culture also gives us guidance about matters of faith and whether we are in control of our own lives or if fate determines our future. What is beautiful or ugly? What is fat or skinny? What is the most appropriate way to express our feelings like grief and joy?

We believe the method to working effectively with clients from other cultures is to critically but unapologetically examine and articulate how one's own cultural experience has developed *expectations* for interacting with others in law enforcement encounters and emergency situations. As a police officer, what are my expectations for interacting with people, say, during a traffic stop? As a paramedic, what are my expectations for how a visit will go with a patient in an emergency? The next step is to try and understand how other people have very different cultural experiences and from these experiences, they may have very different expectations for their encounters with emergency personnel and first responders. Taking into account how the responder's expectations may be different from the client's expectations is critical. Neither party needs to explain away or apologize for their backgrounds, but responders and clients need to bring into their encounters at least some acknowledgement that their expectations may be different. Very often, everyone will make mistakes. At the end of the day, providing culturally competent services is not about changing who we are but understanding and responding to diverse behavioral expectations. It is important to understand that becoming "culturally competent" or "culturally responsive" is *not* about excusing or rationalizing criminal behavior or why victims avoid us or don't report crimes and abuse. Instead, it's about learning how we can provide competent services to meet the unique challenges associated with criminals, victims and other clients with different experiences and cultural backgrounds and to *explain* behaviors without excusing or apologizing for them.

With this background on human culture, what are some of the key implications of multicultural communities for public safety, emergency medical, and emergency management personnel? Foremost, we generally must reexamine and throw out many of our common assumptions. For example, we cannot assume that:

- Emergency responders are the same in all countries;
- Personnel are always trusted in other countries;
- Newcomers should know they don't need bribes;
- Newcomers know that personnel are not corrupt; or
- Concepts of "disasters" are universal.

Let us share one classic example. When Mexican immigrants began arriving in large numbers in the American Midwest two decades ago, they befuddled local and state law enforcement with their refusal to use seat belts and appropriate car seats for young children. In both cases, it seemed, these newcomers were defying common safety sense and the law. However, wearing seat belts and using child car seats in Mexico was the exception, rather than the rule. Indeed, in the 1990s, among the thousands of "counties" or *municipios* in Mexico, only two required car seats for children and only a few more required seat belt use in the front for drivers going out of town. Years after their arrival, Mexican newcomers did adapt to American cultural expectations about car safety, and used seat belts more regularly. In the meantime, public safety personnel found themselves educating these and other newcomers about car safety restraints and handing out tickets to repeat offenders.

Here is another example of how our expectations and assumptions don't always apply. Many refugees in the U.S. and other western nations come from cultures and societies where emergency services like fire and EMS simply don't exist. In some cases, if these services did exist, there were expectations for fees and/or bribes to be paid. In other words, if these services were available, people often avoided them because they could not afford them or involved corruption. It came as a surprise to many fire, emergency medical, and other responders when they were called to provide services, only to be met at the door and told--usually in broken English--"you go!" "we no pay!" or "we no money!"

In other words, these newcomers believed they had to pay cash up front for services or they did not trust the responders. It took a good deal of outreach in schools and among faith communities to educate newcomers about how emergency services work in the US and how they are already paid for by tax dollars.

In addition to these significant cultural differences in expectations and attitudes towards disasters in cross-cultural settings, other implications are occurring as well for responders due to increased diversification of populations in their jurisdictions. For instance, responders now are increasingly dealing with communities where dozens, if not hundreds, of languages are spoken. Even in small rural states like Iowa in the American Midwest, upwards of 200 languages are spoken in the state now due to refugee influxes and global migration patterns for work. Additionally, responders are running into linguistically rare languages or unique dialects where finding an interpreter, anyone, even if by telephone, is almost impossible. Children are also routinely but wrongly being used out of necessity in many emergency settings where language barriers exist. A decline in literacy levels is also being seen in many communities around the world, where families may not even be literate in their native language, let alone that of the host community. Social structures are changing among populations as well, where the family size of many immigrant populations can be larger than that which is common in the majority population. So emergency responders need to take human density and family structural patterns into account when planning for emergencies in some neighborhoods, just as they must be familiar with the local informal leadership structure or tribes, clans, religious groups, ethnic community associations, and other new social entities that now exist in their areas of operation.

3. DEFINING TACTICAL ANTHROPOLOGY

Bottom Line Up Front (BLUF):

• Tactical Anthropology provides skills and techniques for first responders to work effectively in cross-cultural operating areas during emergencies

• Tactical Anthropology uses cultural knowledge to help diverse communities prepare, respond to, and recover from emergencies and keep people safe.

• Like all tools, Tactical Anthropology will be used in some settings and less often in others.

Photo 3.1 Clay County, Minnesota, Sheriff's Department and local search and rescue volunteers check neighborhoods along the Red River in 2009. (Photo by Andrea Booher/FEMA photo.)

In the broadest sense, anthropology is the study of human beings. Cultural anthropology is the study of human culture, language and ethnicity. Applied anthropology takes the methods and approaches of anthropology and applies them to real-world problems. We created the term Tactical Anthropology to apply the perspectives, methods and theory of cultural and applied anthropology to the unique challenges and opportunities faced by our colleagues in law enforcement, emergency medical services, fire, and disaster planning in the United States and internationally when responding to large-scale disasters and emergencies in culturally complex communities.

We have provided training and technical assistance for public safety personnel for decades. We are also first responders. As our communities have become more culturally, linguistically and ethnically diverse, we saw the training and technical assistance needs of our clients and colleagues change. Many of the tried-and-try methods used for decades didn't work any more with a growing number of people in their jurisdictions. Responders and others started asking questions like, "Why don't these people act like everyone else does?"

Among the growing number of challenges diverse populations presented to public safety personnel, we found common issues related to cultural experience and expectations, identity and ethnicity, and language and/or communication challenges. Tactical anthropology provides public safety agencies with the tactics, techniques, and procedures to better meet the needs of culturally diverse, newcomer, and/or marginalized populations within their jurisdictions.

Here is our succinct definition of **tactical anthropology:**

*The utilization of **knowledge about human cultures** in community settings to protect residents, particularly those that are from vulnerable populations, during public safety emergencies, disasters, and large scale crisis situations.*

Public safety practitioners can no longer separate behaviors from the victim's cultural experience or expectations. Here is one way we explain this concept to our colleagues who are first responders. Hippocrates, the founder of western medicine, said thousands of years ago: "It is more important to know what kind of person has a disease than to know what kind of disease a person has." The same can be said in the public safety field. For example, "It is more important to know the culture of the disaster victim than to know the kind of disaster they experienced." Or, "It is more important to know the expectations of our clients than to know what happened to them in an emergency."

Using tactical anthropology and creating Tactical Cultural Asset Teams (T-CATs) uses many of the practices employed in good community policing and public outreach--direct contact with residents, developing relations with faith communities, etc.--but it goes further by admitting and examining the role of human culture and expectations in how diverse people approach public safety issues and how emergency responders can help with these special needs.

Tactical anthropology also recognizes that diverse populations are some of the most vulnerable people in disasters. Not only will we provide more effective and efficient services--which will save more lives--but tactical anthropology will also make jobs safer for law enforcement, EMS, fire and other personnel.

The use of cultural knowledge may be as important, or even more important, than other tactics, techniques or procedures (TTPs) used in public safety and emergency operations. All first responders and emergency managers use sets of tools. In addition to physical tools such as vehicles, EMS equipment and firearms, responders use so-called "soft" tools including specialized skill sets, knowledge and experience. Tactical anthropology is another tool to add to the practitioner's toolbox. This tool provides responders and managers with the skills and perspective to place their work among diverse populations within the context of culture. It helps them see a crisis or emergency as not just another standard or "routine" event, but rather as something that occurs within the unique cultural context of a community and its residents. When it comes to working in diverse communities, "the one size fits all" rule does not apply.

Of course, like all tools, responders and managers will not use the tool of tactical anthropology skills in every situation. EMS personnel will not apply tourniquets to limbs with minor abrasions. The use of certain tools will depend on the nature of the event and the intensity of the situation.

In many situations that require little or no cultural knowledge, its use may actually impede or severely slow down critical services. Many first responders recognize and want to honor or respect certain cultural taboos, but should they do so at the cost of not doing their jobs or saving lives? Absolutely not! We will provide two real examples from our clients' experience. In one example, some colleagues responded to a tragic accident in which a family of Somali Muslims was severely injured or killed. As observant Muslims, most Somalis prohibit males who are not husbands or other direct members of the family to touch females. When EMS personnel arrive at an accident scene where Somali women--in head scarves--lay in the ditch bleeding to death, is it alright for a male responder to touch them to stop them from bleeding to death? Yes! Save lives first, and worry about cultural prohibitions later. Another example comes from some fire colleagues who were called to a house fire in the back of a home of a Burmese family. Typically when visiting families in this culture, one's shoes would be left at the door out of respect. But in an emergency, firefighters must run into a house quickly and safely, and so of course must keep their boots on to save lives and put the fire out. Later, if there is a fire marshall investigation and interviews are conducted in a neighborhood in a non-emergency fashion over the course of several weeks, it might be appropriate at that time to cover your shoes or take them off before meeting with family elders for an extended length of time.

Situations or operations that require a more intensive need for cultural TTPs include:

- Conducting Interviews or Assessments
- Responding to Disasters
- Developing Emergency Management Plans
- Addressing Ongoing Civil Unrest Situations
- Engaging with Key Community Leaders as Partners
- Conducting Community Outreach and Education
- Participating in Search and Rescue Operations

In all of these situations, the use of cultural knowledge is a critical tactical skill. Here is one example from our experience. In many cultures, a family is not just mom, dad and two children but rather a larger, complex network of people for whom cousins or even non-blood relatives have the same status as siblings or parents.

A "household" does not just reside in one location (house, apartment, etc.) but rather the flexible distribution of several real and fictive kin among multiple physical locations. The concept of a "primary address" or "address of record" makes no sense to many people. Also, children in many cultures are not just biological or legally adopted minors but children are often raised by unrelated caretakers. And, although it's difficult to investigate and prove, polygyny (the marriage of one man to more than one woman) can be practiced in some ethnic groups, although it may be illegal in a nation.

First responders to emergency settings must understand the cultural background of the family they are serving, and the cultural context of the situation they are addressing, in order to effectively work within that crisis to help the victims appropriately. To this end, the knowledge of culture is indeed a critical tactical skill that is essential in many disaster, public safety, and emergency response settings.

4. A BRIEF HISTORY OF TACTICAL ANTHROPOLOGY

Bottom Line Up Front (BLUF):

• The U.S. Department of Defense has increasingly recognized the need to understand culture and improve its ability to work in multinational environments during disaster relief, humanitarian aid, provincial reconstruction, and peacekeeping operations.

• Tactical Anthropology applies many of the same concepts and practices of military anthropology, but uses these skills to improve the ability of public safety professionals to respond more effectively to large scale emergencies in culturally complex communities.

Photo 4.1 Members of the Missouri National Guard and the Air Force National Guard stack sandbags to shore up a levee on the Mississippi River, June 2008. (Photo by Jocelyn Augustino/FEMA photo.)

Development of the concept and practice of tactical anthropology emerged from our familiarity and experience with the use of cultural and language assets in United States Department of Defense operations. Indeed, the U.S. Army recognized the need for culturally competent troops and officers decades ago. The Army's Culture and Foreign Language Strategy clearly states that cultural and foreign language "competency involves having sufficient cross-cultural, regional, and foreign language competencies to enable the successful execution of military operations. This not only requires an understanding of the culture and language in a particular area, but an understanding of the implications these considerations have on how operations are conducted." Cultural and geopolitical knowledge has also become a critical aspect of Army leadership:

Cultural understanding is crucial to the success of unified action operations. Leaders should learn the customs, traditions, operational procedures, and doctrine of their unified action partners. To operate successfully in a multinational setting, Army leaders must understand differences in doctrinal terminology and the interpretation of orders and instructions. They must learn how and why others think and act as they do. A multicultural environment requires leaders to keep plans and orders as simple as possible to prevent misunderstandings and needless losses. Dedicated liaison teams and linguists provide a cultural bridge between partners to mitigate some differences, but they cannot eliminate them.

The Army's recognition that culture matters is shared by a growing number of other Western defense forces. The French Army, for example, engages the American approach to culture as it prepares troops for service in Africa. Trainees learn about the great diversity of African cultures and traditions and how to apply this knowledge to winning the "hearts and minds of local villagers in rebellious areas" and training African troops "who are not as deadline-conscious as [the French], who don't work in a linear fashion of schedules and planning, and who don't value controlling processes."

Before troops from the United Kingdom are deployed, they receive mandatory training on the culture of the region where they will serve. Although some degree of "culture clash" between U.K. troops and members of other national militaries and/or local civilians is inevitable, British researchers have found that training about other cultures and languages can make deployments safer by engaging local communities and avoiding local taboos, encourage cooperation among multinational forces, and contribute to soldiers' physical and mental health.

Much of the training and leadership for making the U.S. Army more culturally competent is the mission of Army's Training and Doctrine Command (TRADOC) Culture Center.

The US Air Force also recognized the importance of culture with the creation of the the Air Force Culture and Language Center. Not to be outdone, the U.S. Air Force opened its own Culture and Language Center in 2006 to "a cross-culturally competent Total Force to meet the demands of the Service's dynamic global mission."

The use of cultural assets has been particularly valuable in what the U.S. Army War College refers to as VUCA settings: Volatile, Uncertain, Complex and Ambiguous. Of course, public safety officials in domestic settings are not at war. Yet, there are some similarities in terms of the need for cultural assets in international military settings (higher levels of VUCA) and disasters or civil emergencies that may happen, particularly domestically (lower levels of VUCA). The comparison between military and tactical anthropology in VUCA environments is shown in the table below.

MILITARY MODEL	TACTICAL ANTHROPOLOGY MODEL
Purpose: International Defense Operations	Purpose: Disaster and Emergency Operations (particularly although not exclusively domestically)
Location: Area of Operations	Location: Jurisdictions (city, county, state, regional, federal, etc.)
Goals: · Protect the safety of civilians · Address threats to security · Minimize risk to troops	Goals: · Protect the safety of civilians and victims · Respond to emergencies and disasters · Minimize risk to First Responders
Environment: Higher VUCA Levels	Environment: Lower VUCA Levels
Personnel: Military Units and Defense Agencies; Multinational Forces	Personnel: Emergency Medical Services, Disaster and Emergency Management Agencies, Fire Rescue Units, Public Safety Personnel; Community Policing Units, Relief Agencies; and Other First Responder Organizations

Among the cultural assets employed by the Department of Defense with a particular expertise in working cross-culturally are Military Interpreters and Translators; Cultural Liaisons; Social Scientists; Female Engagement Teams, Provincial Reconstruction Teams; Cultural Support Teams (CST), Foreign Area Officers (FAOs), and others. The use of cultural and linguistic assets are not limited to "downrange" or in the field of military operation. Indeed, we coined the term *Tactical Anthropology* to describe how the methods of cultural asset teams can and should be used in domestic, lower VUCA public safety settings to respond to disasters and large scale emergencies in neighborhoods and communities.

Further Reading

• Juliana Geran Pilon, editor (2009). *Cultural Intelligence for Winning the Peace*. Washington, DC: The Institute of World Politics Press.

• Christopher J. Lamb, James Douglas Orton, Michael C. Davies and Theodore T. Pikulsky (2013). *Human Terrain Teams: An Organizational Innovation for Sociological Knowledge in Irregular Warfare*. Washington, DC: The Institute of World Politics Press.

• Robert A. Rubinstein, Kerry Fosher and Clementine Fujimura, editors (2013). *Practicing Military Anthropology: Beyond Expectations and Traditional Boundaries*. Kumarian Press.

• Robert Albro, George Marcus, Laura A. McNamara and Monica Schoch-Spana, editors (2011). *Anthropologists in the Securityscape: Ethics, Practice and Professional Identity*. New York: Routledge.

References

- Department of the Army, Army Culture and Foreign Language Strategy, 1 December 2009, pg. 3.
- Department of the Army, ADRP 6-22: Army Leadership, 1 August 2012, pg. 5-4
- Henri Bore' (2006). Irregular Warfare: French Army Experience in Africa. *Military Review*, July-August 2006, pages 108-111.
- Tayla Greene, Joshua Buckman, Christopher Dandeker, and Neil Greenberg (2010). The Impact of Culture Clash on Deployed Troops. *Military Medicine*, 175, 12: 958-963.
- Michele Devlin and Mark Grey, "Tactical Anthropology." International Law Enforcement Educators and Trainers Association, Chicago, Illinois, 14 March 2016.

5. WORKING CROSS CULTURALLY

Bottom Line Up Front (BLUF):

• Cultural misunderstanding may be caused by key differences in cultural experiences and expectations.

• One critical difference among cultures is how some cultures emphasize the individual, while others emphasize the extended family, faith community or ethnic group.

• Other key cultural differences may include beliefs in fate and destiny, concepts of time; beliefs about people in authority; decision making processes; community ability to prevent or recover from a disaster; and mechanisms for crisis communication.

Photo 5.1 Disaster responder providing immigrant resident with information translated into Arabic after severe flooding in Fargo, North Dakota, June 2009. (Photo by Samir Valeja/FEMA photo.)

In western nations, most emergency managers, public safety officials, and EMS workers bring their own cultural experiences and assumption as members of "low-context" cultures to their encounters with all clients. Low-context cultures often place an emphasis on individual rights, responsibilities, and achievement. Many lower-context cultures can be found among those populations descended from Western Europe. The core social unit of the culture tends to be the individual and the "nuclear" family. However, a growing number of individuals from "high-context" cultures are increasingly residing in multicultural communities in the West. In many high-context cultures, the primary social obligation and identity is with the group, such as the extended family, the tribe, or the clan. High context cultures can be found around the world, and can include, for instance, many groups of African, Latin American, Native, and Asian descent.

The contrasting obligations and assumptions between professionals (or volunteers) from low-context cultures and clients from high-context cultures has serious implications for public safety encounters and disaster preparedness, response and recovery. How the Ebola crisis of 2014-2015 was handled in the United States provides an excellent example. The Ebola outbreak in Sierra Leone, Liberia and Guinea Ebola placed public health and emergency response personnel on high alert all over the world. Fears that the disease would reach other nations and ignite mass epidemics lead to calls for travel bans from West Africa. Selected hospitals in the United States were designated "Ebola-ready" National and local protocols were initiated to contain the disease based on guidance from medical organization that emphasized protective gear, isolation practices, standardized questions and other technical and operational details but did very little to address patients as cultural beings. Nor did these protocols engage the West African immigrant communities who were already on high alert because they knew that the disease was most likely to enter the U.S. through members of their own families.

When Ebola did arrive with a Liberian man in Texas, public health officials assured citizens that he had likely made contact with only a few people in the United States and they were under observation. But we knew that it was much more likely that the patient--as a member of a high-context culture--had probably contacted dozens of friends and family members in the few short days after this arrival in Texas. Here is how we described this situation in an essay published in *Somatosphere*:

From our perspective, this scenario exposed the over-reliance on medical protocols that screen for diseases in individuals, but often overlook the bigger picture of diseases in families and cultural communities. Patients are often viewed as nameless "vectors," not members of human cultures...Clearly, the perspective, experience and expectations of many of our colleagues in epidemiology around the country emerged from a "low-context" perspective that focuses on individuality. Disease screening too often looks just at the individual patient and ignores broader family and community issues that are important to understand from a "high-context" group-oriented cultural standpoint. This assumption played itself out perfectly when the Centers for Disease Control announced to the world that

the Liberian immigrant first diagnosed with Ebola in Dallas
had only been in the company of, and therefore only
potentially exposed, a handful of people living in his fiance's
apartment. Within days, however, the high-context nature of
Mr. Duncan's culture revealed itself and ultimately public
health workers had to track up to 100 individuals for
potential exposure from a single patient.

In the case of Ebola, emergency managers and public health officials used screening protocols that focused on individuals who travelled to West Africa and returned to the U.S., but not on how the disease might be spread to each other through visits with relatives or friends who might have arrived from West Africa. might arrive via visitors from West Africa. Indeed, members of West African communities understood very well that they were most likely to be exposed to the virus through members of their own families, and in some cases, public health officials were asked to quarantine the family members of West Africans already residing in the US.

Cultural knowledge also helps planners and responders understand that perceptions of risk may result from narratives about vulnerability or that vulnerability—at least in part—stems from how people perceive and express risk. Here is an example: Some community residents may dismiss risk information due to beliefs that the possible consequences of a disaster for their lives (including death) and property loss is beyond human control. People and property will survive a disaster "if God wills it." We refer to these cultures as "fate and destiny" cultures. Other residents may put their full faith and trust in what emergency managers and civic leaders tell them. Local cultural knowledge and experience may also influence perceptions of risk and vulnerability. We have seen many cases where people receive official warnings about approaching floods, and then rely solely in their culture on prayer to protect them from harm. In our experience, most people perceive risk along a spectrum that includes some degree of using both information from official sources; relying on local cultural knowledge; and/or relying on fate, destiny, and faith.

How people use and manage time is also influenced by culture. Cultures that emphasize the importance of timeliness, adherence to timeframes and agendas, and highly structured schedules are called "monochronic" cultures, and can be particularly common among white, Western European descent cultures. In these groups, respecting schedules and other people's time is critical. As many of our monochronic clients like to say, "early is on time and on time is late." But for members of other cultures, time is relative. Schedules are looser. A meeting scheduled for 10:00 may start at 10:20 or even 10:30. These cultures are called "polychronic" because there is no single shared concept or use of time. Time can have different meanings depending on the context. One may be monochronic and get to their job on time but in their personal lives they usually revert to polychronic habits because everyone else in their cultural community are also polychronic.

The contrasting expectations between public safety officials from low-context cultures and residents from high-context cultures accounts for a significant proportion of challenges and frustrations for members of both cultures. But coming in a strong second is contrasting expectations about time.

Indeed, even when many of our clients start to "get" the importance of culture and, say, diverse communication styles, they hit a serious roadblock when it comes to time management. In many respects, timeliness and sticking to schedules is viewed as the most important way people from diverse cultures can show respect for the culture of public safety and other officials with Western expectations. Otherwise, we hear from many service providers, "how else are these people going to make it here?" There are some serious implications to the mono-polychronic divide in the disaster relief field, such as when immigrant or refugee families miss appointments for disaster relief services.

Culture also provides guidance for how to interact with people in authority. These may include bosses, teachers, police officers or emergency managers. For most Americans, respect for authority is scripted, in that there is shared general sense for how the person in authority will communicate with a citizen and how that citizen should talk to the person in authority. There are common expectations for who says what to whom and which type of language is acceptable and what language and/or actions fall are outside the lines. Respect by and for authority may also manifest itself in eye contact or lack of eye contact, tone of voice, and body spacing. American law enforcement officials rely heavily on eye contact to "read" whether people are telling them the truth but in diverse communities, some cultures show respect to those in authority by looking down out of humility and honor.

Members of diverse cultures may also show respect for people in authority but avoiding them or "not wasting their time." In some cases this may relate to fear of retribution, deportation, or a negative experience with corrupt public safety officials in their home country. other cultures, not contacting authorities is how respect is shown. It demonstrates that ordinary people and authorities are not equals. One example that we see quite often in our work with immigrant and refugee populations is that these newcomers are often hesitant to report crime in their communities. In some cases--particularly in high-context cultures--this is a strategy to not embarrass the enclave or drawn unnecessary attention. In many cases, however, these behaviors derive from cultural experiences and expectations that the extended family is responsible for keeping the peace and addressing bad behavior in the community. Reaching out for public safety support can be a sign that the family is a "failure" at protecting its own.

Cultural prohibitions against challenging others with higher rank or authority can have serious consequences. In some cultures, people will not challenge officials or official knowledge even if facts on the ground are more accurate and timely. We have seen this in clinical settings where patients or family members have information about the patient's condition, but it is not given to the physician unless specifically requested. Or the patient or family members disagree with the physician's diagnosis or treatment plan, but these concerns are not expressed to the doctors out of respect for their rank and expertise. We have also seen similar situations when illiterate or poorly educated immigrants or refugees are afraid to question their children's' teachers.

Refusal to question or confront those of higher rank or authority can also have deadly consequences. In 1989, Tan-

Sahsa Airlines Flight 414 crashed on its final approach to the Toncontin International Airport in Honduras, killing 131 passengers and crew. Toncontin is considered one of the most dangerous airports in the world because multiple mountains and ridges must be avoided on the approach. The pilot of Tan-Sahsa 414 deviated from the published flight path leading to the crash. Widespread speculation at the time blamed the pilot for deviating from the prescribed approach, but the co-pilot knew the plane was off course. He did not inform the pilot or insist on a course change out of respect for the senior pilot's rank and authority.

Related to how people interact with people in authority is how they communicate with others in their day-to-day lives. Culture gives people the guidelines for how to express themselves and listen to others. Some cultural communications styles are reserved and quieter, where often what is **not** said is more important than what **is** said. At the other end of the spectrum, some cultures encourage people to directly express their viewpoints, speak more loudly, and communicate physically through hand gestures and closer body spacing. People from more reserved cultures may find people from expressive cultures too aggressive, while those from more expressive cultures may view those from reserved cultures to be boring, secretive, or cold.

All humans experience the same emotions but how they express those emotions is linked to their culture. Here is one example: *grief* is the emotion all people feel usually feel from the death of a beloved family member in a disaster, or a dramatic life change like losing a house to a tornado. *Mourning,* however, is how culture expects members to express that grief, and these cultural norms can vary tremendously among cultures. In some cultures, mourning is shared through silence, while in many cultures mourning is expressed through wailing, dramatic hand and arm expressions, and even the tearing of skin or clothing. Funerals in some cultures are quiet, solemn events where respect is paid in low voices and gentle tears. In other cultures, funerals are celebrations of lives well lived and joy in that the dead person now lives an even better life in heaven.

Much the same can be said about how people feel about emergencies and how they are expected to express not express those concerns. We work with some cultures where the reaction to traumatic events like automobile accidents or cardiac arrests are met with business-like focus: calmly call emergency services, do as much as you can to help victims, see to the successful transfer of victims to appropriate services, and deal with the feelings later. We also work with other cultures where an immediate response to, say, a cardiac arrest is met with loud expressions of concern for the victim and admonishment of emergency responders for "taking so long to get here" while also yelling "Save my father! Oh my God do something!"

Cultures provide guidelines for who are considered "victims" and who "deserves" assistance in crisis situations. In the Upper Midwest United States, there is an spoken but omnipresent rule about who becomes eligible for help and who does not. When an individual or family loses property or suffers an injury or death due to something beyond their control like a tornado, people will appear quickly in large numbers to help, even if they are not friends or relatives. But if an individual or family suffers a loss and its directly or indirectly due to their own bad actions or irresponsible choices, they may not be viewed culturally as legitimate victims and may not deserve help. Examples of these situations include house fires started--even accidentally--by homeowners practicing unsafe behaviors such as plugging in too many appliances into thin extension cords.

Contrasting communication styles have many real-world implications for public safety officials. One example is how to express the potential magnitude of a pending disaster in ways that will resonate with people from different cultures. Warnings about approaching emergencies like hurricanes are designed to sound "official" enough to raise concerns among people in its path but at the same time not create panic. In other words, they are designed to strike a balance between sounding too cautious so that people take the situation seriously but officials cannot be blamed later for over exaggerating the threat if the event turns out to be less dangerous or damaging than predicted. These announcements are intended for general audiences and to reach the most people. But people from different cultures will "read" how crisis messages are presented in different ways, even when they are expressed in a shared language, and may react to these emergencies in very different ways.

References
• Edward T. Hall (1976). *Beyond Culture*. Anchor Books.
• Mark Grey and Michele Devlin (2015). Ebola and the "Global Other" in the United States. *Somatosphere: Science, Medicine and Anthropology.* www.somatosphere.net/2015/01/ebola.net

6. ACCULTURATION, ACCOMMODATION AND CULTURAL AWARENESS

Bottom Line Up Front (BLUF):

- Most of the burden to change behaviors and learn the language of their new host community should be placed on immigrant newcomers.

- Established residents and agencies must also change to some degree to promote accommodation of newcomers and successful integration.

- Reaching out to cultural communities makes the job of first responders easier, safer, and more effective before disaster strikes.

- Not everyone is "cut out" to work across cultures.

- There are five general levels of cultural competence, including cultural blindness and cultural competence.

Photo 6.1 FEMA disaster relief specialist discusses the need for interpreters in Memphis, May 2011. (Photo by Marilee Caliendo/ FEMA photo.)

Accommodation or assimilation? How much do we have to change how we do things? One major purpose of this book is to point out that when it comes to planning for and managing emergencies, we cannot take a "one size fits all" approach. Different populations and diverse cultures may be vulnerable to disasters in very different ways and they may understand and respond to risk in very diverse ways that may contrast markedly from the expectations and experience of most emergency managers and first responders.

But one question often arises at trainings, workshops and conferences where diverse populations are discussed: How much do we (emergency managers, responders, and so forth) have to change what we do for diverse populations and when do they become responsible for doing things our way? These questions often follow statements like "my grandfather from Germany (or any other country of origin) had to learn English, so why don't immigrants and refugees have to learn English?" It's all well and good to translate signs in other languages and reach out to diverse populations, but where does our responsibility end and theirs begin?

These are fair questions. Our general response is that for many first-generation immigrant and refugee newcomers, emergency response agencies will generally need to consider the language and cultural needs of these populations for planning purposes, within the budget and resources available for such response. A good faith effort at reaching out to, and learning from, newcomer populations will not always lead to new or altered services for every new language or ethnicity arriving in most communities. Even in small communities, dozens of languages and cultures may arrive, and mobilizing services in all of these languages and populations is not always practical or affordable.

Rather, good-faith efforts at accommodating diverse populations begins with not assuming that approaches to risk and disaster response that seemed to work for most people in the past will always work for newcomers. Accommodating new and diverse populations means that planners and responders make a reasonable effort to meet the needs of newcomer and diverse populations and this, in the face of limited resources, usually means identifying and working with populations that form a critical mass. In other words, if 5,000 Spanish speakers move to town, it's a reasonable use of resources to translate written materials into Spanish and provide Spanish interpreters at meetings in church basements, at the the hospital, etc. Smaller populations—often speaking rare languages—may not get the same level of service as Spanish speakers who arrived in larger numbers.

The accommodation approach also recognizes that immigrant and refugee newcomers have a responsibility to eventually learn about and respond to risk and disaster management services offered in their new communities. However, this takes time, in some cases even a generation or two. Many established residents of communities in the United States and Europe insist on rapid assimilation on the part of immigrants and refugees. The assimilation model insists that the entire burden of fitting into local society and speaking the local language is with the newcomers, and established residents by and large do not need to change how they have always done things. They will generally feel that the burdern to "fit in" is completely the responsibility of new ethnic groups in the community.

Decades of research on immigration and refugees in North America and Europe have shown that yes, the greatest burden on fitting or integrating into new societies falls on the immigrants and refugees. However, successful communities and public safety officials also recognize that to some extent they must also make some effort to change their own practices—even in very small ways—to make a reasonable accommodation to the linguistic and cultural needs of newcomers. The principle behind this approach is that by reducing risk and providing good services to diverse newcomer populations, everyone in the community or jurisdiction is safer.

Here is one example of this. Research has shown that when public safety and emergency management personnel reach out to diverse populations, members of those populations are more likely to identify and report risks and behaviors that may not only threaten just their ethnic group, but the entire community. During the Ebola outbreak of 2014, West Africans in the United States and elsewhere knew that if or when the virus was brought to the United State or some other nation, the virus would likely be introduced to their communities by relatives and friends from Liberia, Guinea or Sierra Leone. Establishing direct communication with public health officials was critical not only to safeguard the health of West African populations, but to allow these immigrants to serve as lookouts to keep the virus from spreading to the rest of the community.

Is every first responder capable of working effectively in multicultural settings? In an ideal world, the answers would be "yes", but in the real world, some people are better than others at working with people from other cultures who speak different languages. Tactical anthropology, after all, is a critical set of skills that must be learned, and is most effective when it is practiced by first responders that have the kinds of inherent personality traits that are most effective in these settings. In other words, they are trusting, approachable, warm, caring, and welcoming. Most people who launch careers in public safety or emergency management have at least a basic interest in promoting the well-being of humans, or they would not get into the business. Being effective in cross-cultural settings actually can range along a scale, as described in the Cultural Competency Continuum with five different levels (Cross et al 1989). In these jobs, it is rare—but not impossible—to find people who believe in the destruction of other cultures. These people believe in the superiority of their own culture and that other cultures should be marginalized or even destroyed. Unfortunately, history is full of examples where members of one culture sought the destruction or another (think Nazi Germany or ethnic "cleansing" in the Balkans in the 1990s). Hate crimes against individuals or groups of some cultures may even be carried out by individuals along the *cultural destruction* edge of the continuum.

People with *cultural incapacity* viewpoints may not want to destroy people from different cultures. but they do not see the point of learning about others cultures, they tend to see cultural behaviors as "right" or "wrong," and they often become angry when they are asked to learn about or change their attitudes towards diverse cultures. People with this kind of cultural incapacity rely heavily on stereotypes about others.

A recognition of other cultures and a superficial understanding of them are often exhibited by people who are *culturally inattentive or "culturally blind."* They do not deliberately ignore culture. They just don't pay attention to it, by and large. These people see cultural differences as choices rather than unique cultural attributes. They may enjoy tasting new kinds of food or admiring different forms of "traditional" clothing but there is no interest in or understanding of the deeper or hidden aspects of culture. They often become very uncomfortable with or even threatened by thoughts about different values or core beliefs in other cultures. What is the role of men and women? Who is it appropriate to marry? What is "right" and "wrong"? What is the nature of God and what role does God play in one's life?

As in most occupations, many people who work in public safety and emergency services fit into the "culturally inattentive" category. Many may also display some degree of cultural *pre-competence.* They see beyond superficial aspects of culture like food, clothing or holidays and they start to understand some of the deeper cultural differences between themselves and others. Culture is more than just preferences and tastes and there may be serious differences in terms of core values and beliefs. These "pre-competent" people see culture as important but in many cases they find it difficult to understand and may not recognize how culture shapes interactions with others. These folks want to learn more about other cultures, but they often lack sources of information or how to go about asking other people about their cultural backgrounds. There is an interest in changing how they do things to accommodate other cultures but they don't know how.

Most professionals in the so-called helping professions and emergency services fall somewhere between the culturally "inattentive" and "pre-competent" categories. It's our experience that when most people are exposed to, and start to think about, cultural differences, they are often willing to at least start down the road to making some changes in the way they interact with different people.

It is very rare indeed to find people who are fully *"culturally competent"* in any profession. These people understand that diverse beliefs can be, and often times are, deep and intense. They can easily describe why cultural diversity is valuable to them personally and professionally. Human culture impacts everything in life and they understand that culture affects the large and small daily choices that people make. Interactions with others always require some level of cultural competence. Culturally competent people know a lot about at least some cultures other than their own and they actively develop and use a variety of resources for learning more about different cultures, often with the Internet. To some extent, these people are willing to change some of their professional behaviors to meet the needs of others. They know how to be respectful towards members of other cultures while maintaining respect and understanding for their own cultural values. They can successfully negotiate a "middle ground" and accommodate cultural differences when needed.

Reference
•Adapted from "A Guide to Infusing Cultural & Linguistic Competence in Health Promotion Training." National Center for Cultural Competence, Georgetown University Center for Child & Human Development. Based on T.L Cross, B. Bazron, K. Dennis, and M. Isaacs (1989). *Towards a Culturally Competent System of Care, Volume 1. A Monograph on Effective Services for Minority Children Who Are Severely Emotionally Disturbed* Washington, DC: CASSP Technical Assistance Center, Center for Child Health and Mental Health Policy, Georgetown University Child Development Center.

SECTION II:

TACTICAL ANTHROPOLOGY
ON THE JOB

7. PUBLIC SAFETY ORGANIZATIONS

Bottom Line Up Front (BLUF):

• Providing public safety services in multicultural communities presents challenges and opportunities.

• Traditional public safety culture may resist practice changes to meet the needs of culturally diverse communities.

• Typical "diversity" training has sometimes backfired, and bred resentment of the needs of cultural communities.

• Tactical anthropology and cultural awareness training can provide a different approach to teaching public safety professionals about working effectively in multicultural communities, improving the safety of civilians, and minimizing risk to public safety responders in emergency settings.

Photo 7.1 Urban Search and Rescue (USAR) team members work with local law enforcement officers to determine the best course of action in neighborhoods impacted by Hurricane Katrina, September 2005. (Photo by Jocelyn Augustino/FEMA photo.)

Conducting public safety operations in emergency and disaster settings in highly diversified communities presents unique and very real challenges to responders. As communities experience increases in both the number and diversity of new populations, languages, and cultural orientations, public safety agencies will need to adapt to their new working environments in proactive and creative ways.

Professional anthropologists and others have recognized and studied the unique "culture" of public safety for decades. The fundamentals of public safety culture are well documented. Although not monolithic and shared in every public safety force in the world, elements can include a constant regard for danger and maintaining an "edge." These factors tend to sometimes separate public safety officers from the rest of society. This encourages occupational loyalty but also social isolation.

The solidarity and group loyalty of public safety culture presents both its strength and principal weakness. The nature of the job means that officers must rely on each other for physical and even emotional protection. New members are required to demonstrate their willingness to protect their fellow officers. The reward is loyalty, respect, and honor and the willingness of veteran officers to protect newcomers.

Faced with external threats, public safety personnel tend to coalesce and become even more suspicious and isolated, exactly at the time when many communities are experiencing unprecedented diversification. When it comes to public safety operations in multicultural communities, departments often try and recruit diverse individuals to better reflect the community. Other efforts in the US, UK and other nations have involved variations of "diversity training" or "cultural sensitivity training." In our experience, some of these efforts to change public safety culture and "professionalize" the force have actually backfired and led to even greater isolation from general society. In many cases, diversity training has actually led to even more suspicion about diverse communities instead of greater sensitivity and positive engagement.

We developed the concept and practice of "tactical anthropology" largely in response to the dissatisfaction over traditional "diversity training" that has prevailed in some public safety agencies in recent years. This failure has been due largely to the assumption that public safety professionals are inherently biased. Public safety personnel do make mistakes and some are biased against some groups in their communities. But in general diversity training has failed because it does not incorporate culture. Tactical anthropology provides public safety officers with a way to recognize and engage diverse communities during emergencies and disasters in proactive ways, by incorporating cultural knowledge into field operations. Rather than viewing diverse communities as challenges, we emphasize their engagement as a way to enhance effectiveness.

As anthropology specialists, we recognize that knowledge of culture is a tactical skill that can be extremely important to utilize in many disaster response settings. Understanding the cultural context of a community is not an option. It is central to reducing disaster risk for that population, and can help in recovery efforts. Engaging effectively from a cross-cultural standpoint in public safety emergency settings can also reduce the risk of harm to first responders and ultimately contribute to more durable solutions after large scale emergencies. As discussed in Section III of this book, Tactical Anthropology Cultural Asset Teams can be used in public safety organizations to provide a deeper understanding of the area of operations; better plan for disasters affecting these areas; improve community engagement and crisis messaging; arrange for key leader meetings; can operate community coalitions and partners for recovery; and can assist in providing briefings and trainings for other agencies working to address emergencies in socially complex areas of operation that change rapidly.

Further Reading

• R.M Shusta, D.R. Levine, H.Z. Wong, A.T. Olson and P.R Harris (2014). *Multicultural Law Enforcement: Strategies for Peacekeeping in a Diverse Society*. Pearson.

• David E. Barlow and Melissa Hickman Barlow (2000). *Police in a Multicultural Society: An American Story*. Waveland Press.

• Phil Clements (2008). *Policing a Diverse Society* (Blackstone's Practical Policing). Oxford University Press.

• Mary S. Jackson (2006). *Policing in a Diverse Society: Another American Dilemma*. Carolina Academic Press.

• Criminology and Criminal Justice Collective of Northern Arizona University (2009). *Investigating Difference: Human and Cultural Relations in Criminal Justice*. Prentice Hall.

8. EMERGENCY MANAGEMENT AGENCIES

Bottom Line Up Front (BLUF):

• Diverse populations can be especially vulnerable to disasters, due to a variety of factors.

• Cultural knowledge is critical to understand vulnerability among diverse populations.

• How people respond to risk is often driven by culture.

• The four most important aspects of human culture for emergency managers and responders are beliefs, attitudes, values (including religion) and behaviors.

• Religious beliefs and faiths can have a profound impact on risk assessment and preparation.

Photo 8.1 Gathering point for emergency responders in Haiti, 2010. (Photo by Michele Devlin, with permission.)

The use of cultural knowledge has become widely recognized as one of the most important tools in identifying vulnerable populations and preparing for and responding to disasters. The growing body of professional literature on the link between culture and vulnerability has emerged and sessions and/or workshops on identifying and reaching out to diverse populations are now common at professional disaster management conferences across the world.

Cultural experience and expectations play important roles in emergency planning and perceptions of risk. In the United States, for example, this is acknowledged in the Federal Emergency Management Agency (FEMA) principles of the "Whole Communities Approach to Emergency Management" that recognizes how "accelerating changes in demographic trends and technology are making the effects of disasters more complex to manage."

Since Hurricane Katrina, emergency planners have gotten much better at recognizing certain populations are more at risk during disasters but it's another thing to learn how people in these populations perceive and express risk. This is where cultural knowledge is critical. Risk has to do with the likelihood that people or property will be adversely impacted as the result of natural or other hazards. In broad terms, both professional and lay people "define risk in terms of the likelihood that an event of a given magnitude will occur at a given location within a given time and describe the expected consequences that the event will inflict on people and property."

Disasters are generally understood as *events* caused by some natural or man-made (or technical) catastrophe. We have found it more helpful to think of disasters as *processes* rather than events because the social, economic and cultural factors that make disasters social processes existed well before the hurricane or terrorist attack took place. "Although a disaster begins with or is triggered by a natural [or other] event, its effect upon society is grounded in the social system in which it takes place." In 1947, W. Lloyd Warner advised that if you want to learn about a society or culture, watch what happens "when all hell breaks loose." To some degree we agree with Warner, but he implied that before "hell broke loose," there was the normal, day-to-day life of cultures that seem to be doing just fine until they are disrupted by disasters. But we see the social constructs of "normal" life as exactly those processes that make some people more likely to survive disasters than others.

As our fellow anthropologists Oliver-Smith and Hoffman stated it, "Patterns consensus, competition and conflict, tensions between genders, classes, castes, age groups, occupations, all come into focus in disaster situations and provide the opportunity for the expansion of ways to scrutinize generally accepted wisdom regarding social and cultural differentiation." In other words, the strong get stronger and the weak get weaker because things were set up that way before the disaster was triggered by some natural or man-made calamity. Button puts it even more succinctly: "Whether labeled 'man-made' or 'natural,' disaster events highlight ongoing power struggles in society."

It makes sense, then, that the research on natural disasters has largely been based on concepts and theory of vulnerability, particularly of women and children. The generally accepted and shared definition for "vulnerability" was provided by Blaikie et al: "By vulnerability we mean the characteristics of a person or group in terms of their capacity to anticipate, cope with, resist, and recover from the impact of a natural hazard. It involves a combination of factors that determine the degree to which someone's life and livelihood is put at risk by a discrete and identifiable event in nature or in society."

The factors that contribute to vulnerability have been discussed. For instance, impoverished people tend to cluster in densely populated areas and increasingly near coast lines that make them vulnerable to natural events like tsunamis and hurricanes, epidemiological events, and man-made or technological events such as rising sea levels and terrorist attacks. Poverty is more likely to leave women and children at risk during and after disasters because they often do not share the same rights or access as men to jobs, property, financial institutions, post-disaster aid, and health care. Domestic and sexual violence also tend to increase during and after disasters and in the chaos and social dislocation resulting from disasters, as women and children often lose the familial and social support networks that used to provide some degree of protection from violence.

Different populations living in the same community may face similar risks and consequences in terms of the loss of lives, property and livelihoods, but perceptions of risk and vulnerability are understood and expressed through linguistic and cultural "frames" and while maintaining social and power relations. In other words, people are going to perceive risk based on their own cultural experience and expectations and differentiated sources of information.

Many emergency managers struggle with how to communicate risk in highly diverse communities, which can include different languages and literacy levels and a great variety of previous experience with or perceptions of hazards. Although emergency and public safety professionals attempt to communicate risk, the messages are often geared toward English-speaking, literate, and mostly white citizens. These messages are often interpreted by members of other cultures in very different ways than anticipated by authorities and some cases may actually increase risk for some people.

The 2004 tsunami in the Indian Ocean was one of the most devastating disasters in recorded history. In Indonesia alone, the 2004 Tsunami killed 230,000 people and caused $10 billion in damage. Other recent and high-profile Tsunamis occurred in the Solomon Islands in 2007 and in Japan in 2011 during which 18,000 people lost their lives. The fact that many indigenous people living in villages along coasts survived the tsunamis of 2004 and 2007 caught the attention of many researchers and the media. These indigenous people survived because they used "local knowledge" and "ancient stories" to recognize the signs of tsunamis and run for the hills.

According to one media account, the Moka people or "Sea Gypsies" of the Indian Ocean "did not have expensive advanced technology to warn them about the killer waves. They survived merely because of their close relationships with and observation of nature and because they heeded their ancient wisdom and even superstition..." Other people supposedly survived because local folklore taught them when the sea retreated and they could collect fish with their bare hands on the beach a tsunami was imminent. Some researchers referred to such ancient wisdom as "a deep-rooted understanding of place [that] is integrated into the community's practice, culture, and cosmologies"

But not so fast, says anthropologist Matt Lauer. The media tend to romanticize oral traditions about disasters, but in the Indian Ocean oral "histories" often have recent origins and are not embedded in traditional myths and stories. "Indigenous responses to disasters are rarely based entirely on predetermined plans of action spelled out in culturally embedded oral history. Rather, their responses are more accurately understood as intrinsically dynamic and partially improvised. The response is inherently contingent upon and readily hybridizes local and non-local forms of knowledge. Approaches to indigenous knowledge that accommodate oral history and the improvisational, hybridized dimensions have been expressed...as situated practices or strategies."

As Matt Lauer points out, cultural traditions may be part of disaster response but they usually are not the only thing that saves lives. Indeed, in an article in *The New Yorker* magazine, the Sea Gypsy" Moka people from the Surin Islands in Thailand "were unaware of any traditional folklore or legends about tsunamis" Instead, the Moka said they "just saw the wave coming and ran." There is also evidence that the Moka from Lanta Island, Thailand were warned by cell phone calls from family members living on outer islands.

The point is to develop hybrid responses to disaster preparedness and response. "Developing approaches that allow indigenous people to respond and cope with environmental hazards in their own unique ways has the potential to facilitate collaborations between local people and disaster experts."

Human culture is very complex and difficult to define. However, when it comes to understanding the relationship between culture and vulnerability and risk, there are four key components emergency managers and responders need to keep in mind.

Beliefs
Beliefs are non-verifiable but deeply held ideas about what controls the world, including some that relate to ideas about the role of "nature" in relation to risk. Beliefs embody people's explanations of themselves and their place in the world and how the world operates in relation to them. For the vast majority of people, this includes a religious belief...[which] also enable people to have explanations of disasters and ways of behaving that they can reduce risks. (More about religion and risk below.)

Attitudes

Attitudes towards (or perceptions of) risk are the outcome of beliefs in the sense that people may decide that a particular aspect of nature is beyond their control and therefore has to be accepted.

Values

Values influence how people consider that risk should be shared or distributed among different types of people, for instance that an ethnic group [or class of people or religious group] deserves more or less hurt in relation to risk.

Behaviors

Behaviors are the composite outcomes of beliefs, attitudes and values: they are the "operationalized" expression of a particular culture in relation to risk. This includes how people act on their own behalf, in relation to other people, and in regard to outside institutions that may play a role in disaster.

Religion and Risk

For the clear majority of people in the world, cultural beliefs about risk are rooted in religion. We have found emergency managers and first responders don't like to talk about religion, either about their own personal religious beliefs or those of clients and people living in their jurisdictions. One explanation for this reluctance to discuss religion in understanding vulnerability is that it potentially exposes biases in their attitudes towards clients of different religious faiths. Professionals are aware of their potential biases and develop appropriate ways to overcome their personal biases and/or other engage personnel who do not share their biases. In some cases, emergency management workers and first responders view the study of other religions as a threat to their own religious traditions.

E.L.F. Schipper is probably the world's clearest author about this issue. She notes that "One of the first dimensions of vulnerability to be excluded from vulnerability assessments is belief systems...because they are considered too sensitive or taboo to characterize and address from an external perspective. Yet...to omit belief systems from the study of social vulnerability may be to ignore one of the most important drivers of vulnerability to natural hazards."

Religion--like culture--may change across one's lifetime and express itself differently in different social contexts but Schipper tells us there are three generally agreed upon ways that religious perspectives influence causes of hazards and risk and attitudes towards responses:

1. Hazards and disasters cannot be controlled and are a matter of fate. Bad behaviors among humans are punished by God(s) by sending hazards and disasters. From this perspective, the appropriate response is to do nothing because fate cannot be changed. Since God(s) is testing humans the only appropriate response is to not behave in ways that made God(s) send hazards and disasters in the first place.

2. People are victims of hazards and disasters which are caused by God(s). Humans can do nothing since fate cannot be changed. Suffering is necessary for humans and their only appropriate response is praying so losses and deaths will be limited.

3. Disasters are not natural nor caused by God(s). Instead, many hazards may be natural, but disasters are consequences of vulnerabilities caused by social, economic and political factors. God(s) has nothing to do with disasters because human culture and

institutions make some people more vulnerable to risk than others. Therefore, the best response is to reduce the factors and conditions under which people because vulnerable in the first place and build technical and infrastructure defences. As Schipper states, "Religious beliefs often focus on hazards or disasters but rarely consider *vulnerability* to them as a cause of disasters.

It is important to note at this juncture that the vulnerability approach to understanding disasters and disaster response does not attempt to challenge or change people's religious beliefs. Rather, vulnerability research takes into account the role of religion and other cultural factors in what makes people vulnerable in the first place. It's our experience that emergency managers and other responders are most uncomfortable talking about two things in assessing risk in their communities: class (socioeconomic status) and religion. Between these two, however, the discourse about religion and the degree to which one's beliefs make them vulnerable to disasters is a taboo subject. But we argue--like Schipper and many other colleagues--that religion has to be discussed in any meaningful assessment of risk and vulnerability.

Members of some populations may distrust sources of data and information about risk and instead put more faith in fellow members of their cultures or extended families. When official sources of information about risk are not trusted, members of some populations will rely on each other for information. This can be helpful but in many cases the information can make matters worse and leave some people even more vulnerable to hazards. One example of this is the reluctance of many of our refugee clients to call 911 because of persistent rumors that this can result in their children being taken away from them.

For these reasons and more, tactical anthropologists are critical when working in the disaster relief field. They can provide urgently needed, in depth cultural knowledge about key populations in the area of operations, including languages spoken, main ethnic populations, demographic information, cultural beliefs and attitudes, and socio-economic information on the population. They can help predict risk, mitigate harm, and ultimately assist in community development after disasters, and are urgently needed to provide this often-overlooked information in planning for each of the phases within the disaster cycle.

Further Reading

* Deborah S.K. Thomas, Brenda D. Phillips, William E. Lovekamp and Alice Fothergill, editors (2013). *Social Vulnerability to Disasters.* New York: CRC Press.
* Ben Wisner, Piers Blaikie, Terry Cannon and Ian Davis (2003). *At Risk: Natural Hazards, People's Vulnerability and Disasters.* New York: Routledge.
* Greg Bankoff, Dorothea Hilhorst and George Frerks (2004). *Mapping Vulnerability: Disasters, Development and People.* New York: Routledge.
* Jaimie Hicks Masterson, Walter Gillis Peacock, Shannon S. Van Zandt, Himanshu Grover, Lori Feild Schwarz and John T. Cooper Jr. (2014) *Planning for Community Resilience: A Handbook for Reducing Vulnerability to Disasters.* Island Press.
* UNC Institute for the Environment and MDC, Inc. (2009). *Community Based Vulnerability Assessment A Guide to Engaging Communities in Understanding Social and Physical Vulnerability to Disasters*

References

•Sarah Fisher. "Violence Against Women and Natural Disasters: Findings from Post-Tsunami Sri Lanka," *Violence against Women* 16, no. 8 (2010), 904.

•Anthony Oliver-Smith and Susana M. Hoffman. "Why Anthropologists Should Study Disasters." In *Catastrophe and Culture: The Anthropology of Disaster*, ed. Susanna M. Hoffman and Anthony Oliver-Smith. (Santa Fe: School of American Research Advanced Seminar Series), 10.

•Gregory V. Button, "Popular Media Reframing of Man-Made Disasters," In *Catastrophe and Culture: The Anthropology of Disaster*, ed. Susanna M. Hoffman and Anthony Oliver-Smith. (Santa Fe: School of American Research Advanced Seminar Series), 146.

•P.M. Blaikie, T. Cannon, I. Davis and B. Wisner. *At Risk: Natural Hazards, People's Vulnerability and Disasters* (London: Routledge, 1994), 9.

•McAdoo, Brian G., Andrew Moore, and Jennifer Baumwoll (2009) Indigenous Knowledge and the Near Field Population Response During the 2007 Solomon Islands Tsunami. *Natural Hazards* 48(1):75

•Matthew Lauer (2012). Oral Traditions or Situated Practices? Understanding How Indigenous Communities Respond to Environmental Disasters. *Human Organization* 71(2):176-187. Griswold, Eliza (2005) Sea Gypsies. *The New Yorker*. URL:<http://www.newyorker.com/archive/2005/01/24/050124ta_talk_griswold> (March 10, 2011)

•Ziegler, Alan. D., Poh P. Wong, and Carl Grundy-Warr (2009) Still Vulnerable to Killer Tsunamis. *Science* 326(5957): 1188-1189.

•Terry Cannon (2015). Disasters, Climate Change and the Significance of "Culture." In *Cultures and Disasters: Understanding Cultural Framings in Disaster Risk Reduction*, F. Kruger, G Bankoff, T. Cannon, B. Orlowski and E.L.F Schipper. New York: Routledge, pg. 93

•E. Llisa F. Schipper (2015). Religions and Belief Systems: Drivers of Vulnerability, Entry Points for Resilience Building? In *Cultures and Disasters: Understanding Cultural Framings in Disaster Risk Reduction,* F. Kruger, G Bankoff, T. Cannon, B. Orlowski and E.L.F Schipper. New York: Routledge.

9. FIRE, EMERGENCY MEDICAL SERVICES AND SEARCH OPERATIONS

Bottom Line Up Front (BLUF):

• The acute nature of fire, EMS, and search and rescue work discourages closer examination of victims' cultural backgrounds.

• Like the police, practitioners of firefighting, emergency medical services. and search and rescue operations generally do not always see how cultural knowledge can help them to do their jobs better.

• Differences in expectations for--and behaviors during-- encounters with the public may have significant impact on outcomes.

Photo 9.1 Emergency medical care for low-income villagers in India, 2011. (Photo by Michele Devlin, with permission.)

Professional and volunteer First Responders all have in common the fearless urge to rush to the scene and save lives and protect property. This does not make them reckless. but rather they thrive on the sense of urgency and vitality of the mission. They are willing to risk injury and work in unstable and often dangerous conditions. When others run away from difficult situations, first responders run to them. Despite their reputation for being courageous, first responders also often experience emotional trauma when they witness the loss of human lives or experience social dislocation.

First responders have in common with public safety professionals the fact that their jobs are often acute. They get the call for service, arrive on the scene, perform the functions necessary to do the job, and--like the police--close the case and return to base or home. This acute approach to firefighting and prevention, emergency medical services (EMS), mass casualty operations, and missing person searches also means first responders often don't believe that interacting with patients and victims and their families is in their job descriptions. They often view themselves as technical operators, not as human engagement specialists. We see this time and time again in crises to which volunteers and professionals respond. This scenario is expressed with statements like these: "Our job is to stabilize and transport the patient. Why do we need to talk to their families?" "We are supposed to put out the fire and secure the scene. I don't get paid to talk to people." Or, "Why are we wasting resources and personnel interviewing the extended family members of a missing person when those people should be out looking for her!" In many cases, we have seen firefighters and EMS providers walk right by the very families whose house was on fire or whose loved one had a cardiac arrest. It's almost as though the "rescue" personality means responders should not get distracted talking to other people.

This is where a tactical anthropology approach can make a difference. When responders have already convinced themselves that the human context within which they work is irrelevant or that human culture does not matter for their job, emergency services are less effective.

When first responders presume all patients and victims view crises and emergencies with the same cultural lens, it precludes a series of often critical points of information and some case may make matters worse for the people responders are trying to protect.

Different ethnic groups organize themselves in potentially very different ways. This is the case among Native American communities in the USA. For some tribes, membership is based on strict bloodlines. For other tribes, eligibility for enrollment may looser and based just on a person's declaration of heritage. Also, people may also enroll in more than one tribe. Membership or enrollment in a recognized tribe is one thing but how tribes organize themselves internally can vary tremendously. Most outsiders--including law enforcement and first responders--bring their own cultural assumptions about how communities are organized to their encounters with Native American communities and this is often a mistake.

Although people may belong to or enroll in the same tribe, membership in certain clans within the tribe may be more important for economic or political reasons. Clans are basically large families the members of which claim a common origin from an individual ancestor or family. Clans in Native American communities are often associated with status or power, for example only members of certain clans may be chiefs or tribal council members. In some cases, only members of certain clans may perform key rituals. Rivalries between clans can be long standing and members of clans protect other members from the actions of members of other clans.

Outsiders are rarely allowed to see how clan rivalries work but when outsiders are giving access to that information, they must handle it very carefully. One example includes bringing in first responders from outside the tribe to look for missing persons on tribal lands. Most searchers and search managers focus on techniques and strategies. However, the tactical anthropology approach looks deeper to uncover the role of culture and how tribes organize themselves. Searchers in Indian country have to navigate the context within which the person is likely to be found and, most importantly, by whom.

Here is one example from a search event on a Native American reservation in the U.S.in which we were involved. A female tribe member in her early thirties was reported missing by her family and after a few days, and the tribal police called in a professional search and rescue team. It was winter and unless the missing person had travelled away from the reservation, she was presumed dead. The Searh and Rescue (SAR) team hoped to look for a live person but in reality, the team knew they were looking for the subject's body.

What made this search anything but routine, however, was the real reason outsiders were brought in for the search. It was not just that they had certified skills and experience, but mostly because they were not members of the tribe. In other words, if someone was going to find her body, it had to be someone from outside the tribe. Why? Because the subject was a member of one clan but the person suspected in her possible murder was from a rival clan. If someone from the subject's clan found her body, it would inflame suspicions against the member of the other clan who was suspected of killing her. If a member of the second clan found the subject's body, it proved members of the clan knew that one of their members killed the victim, knew where to find her body and attempt to cover for their clan members behaviors. A leader of the SAR team reportedly asked a leader of tribe point blank, "Do you need one of us to find her rather than a member of the tribe?" To which the tribal leader responded, "That's why you are here."

From a firefighting and investigation perspective, training is usually technically robust but rarely, if ever, includes training on the victims or perpetrators of fires or their cultural backgrounds. A tactical anthropology approach, however, could help firefighters and investigators do their jobs better. Here are a few examples.

Fire prevention:
   •Don't assume everyone from immigrant and refugee populations has had previous education on how to avoid fires by not overloading outlets with multiple extension cords.

   •Do not assume they have had previous experience using gas or electric stoves or space heaters.

   •In businesses owned and operated by cultural newcomers, do not assume they are familiar with building codes and fire prevention practices.

Fire awareness:
   •Do not assume knowledge about smoke detectors or the need for fire extinguishers in houses or apartments.

Emergency Medical Services:
Emergency medical service providers also tend to treat patients as

cases. While it is understandable to the immediate task at hand is to stabilize the patient and possibly transport the patient to the hospital, not all patients and their families are the same. The idea that a patient is a "case" and the EMS encounter is "acute" is not universal. The challenge, again, is to examine one's own cultural experience and expectations and how those expectations and experiences may differ from those of people from other cultures.

The acute or short-term nature of most EMS encounters discourages in-depth inquiries about patients. This can have disastrous or even deadly consequences. Even taking a few more minutes to talk to victim's families and/or bystanders instead of rushing to a diagnosis is critical. As Adam Benforado points out, humans are "masters at jumping to conclusion based on an extremely limited amount of evidence. The automatic processes in our brain quickly take in the scene and then reach a conclusion about the victim based on what is right in front of us, without considering what we might be missing. Ambiguity and doubt are pushed to the side."

A case in point was John Doe, a middle-aged white man found collapsed on a sidewalk in suburban Washington, DC with minor head wounds but labelled ETOH, EMS speak for intoxicated. Fire and EMS personnel on the scene smelled alcohol on the man's breath and vomit on his clothing and concluded that he was drunk and tripped on the sidewalk hitting his head in the process. They did not conduct a thorough examination. Police arriving at the scene accepted the conclusion the man was just drunk and they did not secure the scene, conduct a search of the area or talk to witnesses. "When the lead officer on the case was asked if he had filled out the mandatory incident report, he replied, "No, not for a drunk." As the victim had no identification on him, he was labelled John Doe ETOH (the abbreviation for ethyl alcohol or ethanol) and transported to a local hospital to "sleep it off." Only when an attending nurse noticed a growling snore, "posturing," unequal and unresponsive pupils did hospital personnel recognize serious neurological injuries and he was rushed to surgery. He died six days later. Although the victim had been casually drinking at a social event, he was in fact the victim of an assault and robbery.

As responders and medical personnel were just dealing with another "drunk," they went through motions. But when the victim was identified as David Rosenbaum, a highly respected reporter and editor at the Washington Post, this was no longer just a case of ETOH. Newspaper articles and official inquiries followed. The case also prompted changes in EMS, fire and police procedures.

EMS personnel will often respond to health issues that may be described in terms of symptoms (shortness of breath, disorientation, unexplained bodily aches), but among refugee populations these symptoms can be the signs of trauma. Refugees experience trauma when they become refugees and are forced to leave their homes. Trauma is also experienced when crossing international borders, finding and settling into refugee camps, and waiting--often for years--for an opportunity to resettle in a third country like Australia or the U.S.

It is often presumed by EMS and other personnel that once refugees reach the safety of the new country, they will realize how lucky they are and their their trauma will subside. But in many cases, expectations for their new lives are often thwarted and life in a new country brings on new levels of trauma. These traumatic experiences often manifest themselves in physiological ways that prompt calls for EMS. According to Doctors without Borders, a medical organization that serves refugees around the world, the most common psycho-social symptoms and signs that are observed in refugees across cultures include:

- anxiety disorders
- depressive disorders
- suicidal thoughts and attempts at suicide
- anger, aggression and violent behaviour
- drug and alcohol abuse
- paranoia, suspicion and distrust
- somatic presentation of psycho-social problems
- insomnia

This is where a tactical anthropology approach can make a difference. It will be critical to learn from the patient and his/her family their experience as immigrants and refugees and the degree to which their medical conditions are the result of trauma. Tactical Anthropology specialists can help explore the answers to some of the most important questions for these patients, such as how were these conditions viewed and treated back in the home country; what kinds of stigma may exist in the community among these mental conditions; how do individuals display stress or extreme trauma; and are their local traditional healers that could be of assistance in these situations.

Further Reading
•Gary Ludwig (2008). Growing Diversity: Do race & culture matter in EMS? *Journal of Emergency Medical Services*, October 31. http://www.jems.com/articles/print/volume-33/issue-11/administration-and-leadership/growing-diversity-do-race-cult.html

•Lynne Dees (2007). Culturally Competent Care in the Emergency Medical Services. *Texas EMS Journal*, July/August. https://www.dshs.texas.gov/emstraumasystems/JA07CulturallyCompetentCare.pdf
•Washington State Department of Public Health (2008). *Multicultural Awareness for Prehospital EMS Professionals.* www.doh.wa.gov/Portals/1/Documents/Pubs/530091.pdf
•Michele Devlin and Mark Grey (2014). *Navigating the Human Terrain of Search and Rescue Operations*. National Search and Rescue Conference, Woodcliff Lake, NJ.

Reference
•Adam Benforado (2016) *Unfair: The New Science of Criminal Injustice.* New York: Crown Publishing, Pg 10.

10. INTERNATIONAL DISASTER AGENCIES

Bottom Line Up Front (BLUF):

●Disaster response organizations that take a one-size-fits-all approach for relief can not respond to local cultural considerations in a community.

●Rapid cultural assessment of local populations using tactical anthropology methods will inform relief workers about the cultures, ethnicities, languages, and demographic patterns of disaster victims that are critical for planning and response purposes.

●Understanding local economies and class structure will assure relief resources are distributed in such a way as to benefit as many people as possible regardless of status prior to the disaster.

Photo 10.1 Row of International Red Cross tents in Haiti after the Port au Prince earthquake in 2010. (Photo by Michele Devlin, with permission.)

Large-scale disasters across the globe are often covered by the media. In addition to reporting the number of casualties and the magnitude of the disaster, the media also report on the response of international relief agencies. The media usually focus on the larger, well-known agencies like the International Red Cross/Red Crescent, Oxfam, and *Medicins sans Frontieres* (Doctors without Borders) but dozens of smaller, less famous agencies from countries around the world also respond to global disasters large and small.

In general, the work of disaster relief agencies is praised by the media, citing the rapid and mass movement of relief supplies and equipment and the selfless sacrifice of aid workers. The media also very often characterize relief work as apolitical, even noble, as aid workers and volunteers "roll up their sleeves, pull together, and put prior political and social divisions on the shelf. This is sometimes described as a post-disaster utopia, wherein formal rules and regulations are set aside, the usual distinctions between rich and poor are disregarded, and people feel an unselfish concern for the welfare of others." However, social scientists are quick to point out that disasters and disaster relief efforts are anything but apolitical, arguing that disasters are often the direct result of the surrounding political, social and economic environment. Dr. Kathleen Tierney is a sociologist who studies major disasters including Hurricane Katrina. She argues that politics drive how important decisions are made in recognizing hazards, determining risk and responding to disasters. For example, politics drive the way hazards are considered social problems that may require some form of governmental response. Who develops plans for mobilizing personnel and other resources to disasters? Which agencies determine which victims of a disaster will be the first to receive aid and in what form?

Some social scientists argue that politics get worse after major disasters and during reconstruction efforts, particularly at large-scale disasters involving multinational responses. Here is one example: After the massive 2004 Boxing Day tsunami in the Indian Ocean, observes Lisa Smirl, "Humanitarian reconstruction after a large-scale natural disaster has become a key site of international politics: a site where global assumptions, relationships, and responsibilities are negotiated, solidified and questioned."

We also argue that in addition to politics, international aid agencies too often disregard local cultures, social relations, history and economic conditions. This is where using a tactical anthropology approach can make a difference. Instead of assuming that one set of approaches to providing post-disaster aid will work in every country or community, tactical anthropology provides methods to look at the local cultural context to make relief efforts more effective and efficient.

Here is an example. Typhoon Haiyan (also known as Super Typhoon Yolanda) was the strongest storm ever recorded at landfall. When Haiyan hit the Philippines in November 2013, at least 6,300 people were killed and there was massive destruction of housing and infrastructure. Several nations sent millions of dollars, aid supplies and other resources including military personnel and equipment and hospital ships. Among the many well-known non-governmental organizations (NGOs) responding to the disaster were the American Red Cross, Mercy Corps and Catholic Relief Services.

But in the disaster response business, bigger does not always mean better. Indeed, large NGOs tend to be less flexible than their smaller, less well known counterparts and they tend to bring the same assumptions and practices to every disaster scene and show little regard for local culture and social systems. This was certainly the case in the Philippines in the wake of Haiyan. Many of the large aid agencies took the approach that can be phrased this way: "they already know what the locals need because the same methods worked in all of the other places they worked. Because our practices are universal, we already know the locals will be grateful for whatever we do for them."

Local populations in hard-hit cities like Tacloban were grateful that foreign aid workers arrived to help with local recovery, including many who left their homes and families during the Christmas Holidays to respond. However, as large NGOs already assumed what local people needed in terms of food and shelter, the region became saturated with rice and other foods, tents and blankets to the point where local facilities could not store all of the arriving aid and local officials found themselves scrambling to distribute aid to their communities in equitable ways. But surpluses were often unevenly distributed to local elites. In some cases, the storage and distribution of aid came under unscrupulous and even criminal organization as was also experienced in Haiti after the 2010 earthquake.

With a one-size-fits-all approach, the larger NGOs also did not take into account local politics, social organization and culture. Ethnicity and group identity were assumed to be irrelevant. After all, disaster victims all shared the same needs. But this approach failed to take into account how ethnic, social and class relations prior to the disaster don't go away just because their physical communities are destroyed. Instead, status issues in the communities established before disasters strike are usually made worse after disasters. Class status plays out in access to aid workers and supplies. Ethnic and social relations that made some people at higher risk than others not only led to greater prevalence of death or injury but to delayed or even denied access to shelter, food and other forms of assistance. Also, differences in languages were often ignored, citing the irrelevance of language in determining the assumed universal needs of disaster victims. Smaller NGOs from the Philippines and other nations took rather different approaches surveying the economic and cultural scene of the communities they served before and after the disaster, and then determined the best course of action. In other words, they used a tactical anthropology approach and made no assumptions about what locals needed and how to best serve them.

One other major difference among NGOs was how they respond to disasters in traditional ways by handing out blankets, food and tents or providing opportunities for victims to determine the type of aid they identify themselves. That is, instead of assuming what victims need, let them figure that out on their own terms and provide the resources to obtain them through cash transfer programs.

One NGO that takes this approach is the Tzu Chi Foundation, a Buddhist aid society based in Taiwan but with offices around the world. In the Philippines after Haiyan, two very different approaches to recovery were taken. The first was to provide emergency cash aid of 8,000 to 15,000 Philippine Pesos depending on the size of the families. Instead of handing material aid and food to victims, Tzu Chi empowered people to determine their own needs and obtain shelter and supplies depending on their personal experience and needs. Beyond emergency cash payments, the second approach from Tzu Chi that differed from most other aid agencies was the organization of a large-scale cash-for-work program in Tacloban. This plan employed up to 31,000 people each day for about two weeks to clean up debris. Not only did this program clean out thousands of tons of debris, it also kick started the local economy. Instead of being left with warehouses of unused material and food, the local populations could use their cash incomes reestablish their lives and livelihoods in ways that made sense to them and restore ethnic and social relations similar to those before the storm. In some cases, emergency cash payments and clean-up wages even helped some locals with relatively low status before the Typhoon to improve their status to levels unlikely before the storm.

Tactical anthropologists can therefore play a key role not just in domestic emergency response, but in international aid operations as well. They can conduct rapid community assessments and explore the demographic patterns within the area of operations. They can determine primary ethnic populations, language spoken, cultural values and attitudes that are critical for recovery and response, key leaders, preferred emergency messaging venues, and other important factors that must be understood by relief agencies. Tactical anthropologists can help brief this information to their own organizations and collaborative units, as well as serve as key points of contact with cultural communities that are experiencing short and long-term disasters.

Further Reading
●Damon P. Coppola (2015). *Introduction to International Disaster Management*. Butterworth-Heinemann.
●David A. McEntire (2014). *Disaster Response and Recovery: Strategies and Tactics for Resilience*. Wiley.
●John Hannigan (2012). *Disasters without Borders*. Polity Press.

SECTION III:

TACTICS, TECHNIQUES AND PROCEDURES (TTPs)

TTP 1: DEVELOPING TACTICAL CULTURAL ASSET TEAMS (T-CATs)

Overview:

As is clear from the introductory sections of this training manual, Tactical Cultural Asset Teams (T-CATs) are needed now more than ever in many law enforcement, homeland security, emergency management, first response, and related public safety settings. Depending on the size of a jurisdiction, budget realities, and the level of cultural complexity in a community, T-CATs can be developed to meet the needs of a public safety agency and the community it serves. They can be large or small. They can operate on a well-funded permanent basis around the clock, or just activated when needed on a smaller scale as part of the regular job duties of team members. They can be made up of security professionals as well as lay community representatives as appropriate, with a fluid mix of personnel as needed. T-CATs can include public safety professionals from the host agency with excellent community engagement skills, law enforcement interpreters, cultural liaisons from particular populations of interest, key community leaders, anthropologists from local universities, and others with outstanding skills in communication, human interaction, and a passion for cross-cultural interaction and analysis. T-CAT members must be willing to work with populations that are often marginalized by others and sometimes viewed as labor-intensive burdens in emergency response. They must be as comfortable talking with ethnic market owners as they are with visiting homeless meal sites or crowded refugee apartment buildings. Quite simply, T-CAT members thrive in working with chaos, where the challenge of responding to emergencies and crisis situations is amplified by language, cultural, and financial barriers. T-CAT members have excellent street "cred" and smarts, but are also enthusiastic book learners and listeners about the traditions and values of cultures.

Tactics, Techniques, and Procedures:

●Develop a T-CAT that is an appropriate size for your agency, and scale it to fit your budgets, needs, and resources over time. Some T-CATs can be ad hoc and operate as needed in a crisis, particularly in their early months of operation, just as CART (child abuse response teams), V-CAT (violent crime apprehension teams) and special operations teams do in many agencies. As the need grows and the value of a T-CAT is seen by an agency, the size of the team can increase and the services it provides can be more regular and on-going.

●Carefully vet and select members of the T-CAT. A varied skill set is needed. One of the most important skills is excellent human interaction and cross-cultural engagement interests. A member can always be trained, for instance, on the more obscure points of a culture, but it is difficult, if not impossible, to train people to have the right personality to conduct intensive multicultural operations. Enthusiasm, genuine cultural curiosity, and compassion for underserved populations are also highly desired traits for T-CAT members.

●Include both male and female members on tactical cultural anthropology teams. Due to the important role that gender plays in many cultures, some interactions will be better suited for men or women, depending on the members of a cultural community in which a T-CAT is engaged.

●Likewise, include T-CAT members from a range of ages. Younger staff can be helpful in working with culturally diverse youth, while many adults in diverse communities will often prefer culturally to interact with middle-aged or senior representatives from a public safety agency, particularly if they are tribal or clan elders.

•Determine the most appropriate area of operations for your T-CAT. In some larger organizations in highly complex urban settings, a T-CAT may be most appropriate to be situated in an individual first response agency. In other cases, particularly in smaller communities, a regional or multijurisdictional T-CAT may be more appropriate, and it can convene less often for operations.

Situational Tactical Exercise:

Consider your own area of operations. Complete the following template to guide your thoughts in the development of a T-CAT that would suit the needs in your jurisdiction. Mark those responses that are most appropriate for your planning needs.

Tactical Cultural Asset Team Planning Guide

Area of Operations where Tactical Cultural Asset Assistance is Needed	City County Regional State/Province Multi-State/Province National Cross-Border
Potential Location for T-CAT	Agency Only Multi-Agency Multi-Jurisdictional Regional Cross-State or Cross-Border
Estimate of T-CAT Frequency of Operations	Ad Hoc or Only as Needed Periodically Often Very Frequently
Possible Staffing Scenarios	Volunteers Reserves Part-time Paid Staff Full-time Paid Staff Other
Potential Size of T-CAT	3-5 Members 6-12 Members Greater than 10 Members
Membership Skill Set Needed by T-CAT within Its Specific Jurisdiction	Public Safety Homeland Security Fire Emergency Medical Services Emergency Management Anthropologists Cultural Liaisons Other
Types of Emergencies in Jurisdiction	Tornadoes Floods Hurricanes Earthquakes Other Natural Disasters Civil Unrest Other
Ongoing Training Needs Provided to or by the T-CAT	Cross-Cultural Interpretation and Communication Understanding a Specific Cultural Population Ethnographic Interviewing Engaging with Key Leaders Other

Photo TTP 1: Multi-agency team members from FEMA, the National Weather Service, SBA and other agencies work together to gather community needs information after a major disaster. (Photo by Sharon Karr/FEMA photo.)

TTP 2: IDENTIFYING BUDGET NEEDS AND FUNDING RESOURCES

Overview:

The need for culturally effective public safety operations in first responder fields is recognized by professionals in many occupations. This recognition, however, is often particularly strong after a failed mission or poorly handled response with individuals that are from culturally complex communities, due to significant language barriers, misunderstanding of the cultural practices of the population affected, or other such challenges. During briefings or "after action reports", many first responders often mention the need for greater language and cultural understanding by their force when working with a particular community in order to minimize casualties. These reflections can serve as powerful opportunities to advocate for the development of a T-CAT in an organization and to pursue funding for their support. Unfortunately, too few public safety agencies plan proactively for addressing cross-cultural needs in emergencies, and wait until a crisis has happened or a mission has failed before thinking about how to better fund personnel and supplies to address these needs.

As discussed previously in the book due to the changing populations that many first responders now serve, Tactical Cultural Asset Teams are needed in many public safety settings. They are no longer optional resources far down on a wish list, but rather can be a critical tactical asset to develop for an agency. Fortunately, from a budgetary standpoint, T-CATs can take a variety of forms depending on the needs in a community and the resources of the public agency operating it. They can be large or small. T-CATs can operate on a well-funded permanent basis around the clock, or just be activated when needed on a smaller scale as part of the regular job duties of team members. They can be made up of security professionals as well as lay community representatives as appropriate, with a fluid mix of personnel as needed. Funding and budgetary considerations for their operations are presented below:

Tactics, Techniques, and Procedures:

●Use a fluid budgetary model for the development and management of T-CATS. Operational supplies and human resources can expand or shrink as needed based on operations, public safety concerns, and the ever-changing level of cultural complexity in the public safety agency's area of operations.

●The budget for tactical cultural anthropology assets can vary, based on the size. For T-CAT operations in large urban mega-cities that are culturally complex on a permanent basis, seek to utilize or develop "hard money" funding sources or permanent personnel and resource lines at the agency level. Public safety personnel can be full- or part-time paid staff for these operations.

●For mid- to smaller-size agencies, use different funding models. Draw upon existing staff in an agency that can come together only when needed for tactical operations in culturally complex neighborhoods. This model is often used already by agencies for child abductions or (CART-Child Abuse or Abduction Response Teams) or Violent Crime Response Teams (V-CATs)

●If personnel funding is limited, consider using Reserve Police Officers, volunteer firefighters, and other on-call community members as needed, and develop them into a voluntary T-CAT that operates during emergencies. In their downtime, this completely voluntary team can focus on collecting information, gathering supplies, and developing resources and referrals for cultural needs by the departments. These reservists do not necessarily need to be certified law enforcement officers, but could be supplemental professional anthropologists and other cultural specialists for a department.

●Conduct briefings for entities that fund public safety agencies about the need for tactical cultural assets. Surprisingly, many county supervisors, city mayors, and even state legislators have little understanding of how quickly the service population in an area of operations may be changing. They must hear this information directly from Fire Chiefs, Police Chiefs, Public Safety Commissioners, and other heads. These administrators must actively advocate for increased funding for cross-cultural work.

•Consider developing a collaborative funding model for T-CAT operations in smaller communities. For example, there may be little full-time need for this kind of service in a small fire department or a local police agency in a rural community. However, each of these smaller agencies could contribute a portion of the funding, personnel, or equipment needed to make a regional T-CAT where needed, or in some cases, even a statewide T-CAT in rural, sparsely populated states.

•If hard money is limited in an agency, consider seeking "soft money" or grant funding for operations. Grants will typically support personnel, but would need to be resubmitted or renewed annually or every few years to keep those personnel lines operating. So these funding sources are "softer" and not as reliable as hard money that is budgeted annually by an agency to operate a T-CAT. Sources of grant personnel funding can come from state public safety and homeland security agencies, as well as from federal grant application sources that are more competitive and highly challenging to write. Conduct grant searches online for applications that seek to address diversity topics, cultural awareness, interpretation, disparity reduction, and related topics.

•Seek grant money and external funding to support the supplies and equipment needed for T-CAT operations. Because equipment and supplies can last years, grant funding is an excellent mechanism to purchase training gear, communication go-kits, telephonic interpretation contracts, T-CAT vests, off-road or four-wheel-drive modes of transportation to remote areas, and other possible needs. Local community foundations, casino grants, and individual donors can be very helpful in providing funds for these types of operations. For-profit corporate foundations can also be useful, particularly if they are from larger anchor companies that often rely on immigrant or refugee workers that contribute to high levels of cultural complexity in a jurisdiction.

• Seek donations of actual equipment to assist the T-CAT team. Sometimes it is easier for organizations to donate supplies and equipment, rather than cash, to support first responders. Consider approaching local dealers of fat tire or mountain bikes, for instance, to donate to a T-CAT that operates heavily on gravel roads or flood prone regions.

• Partner with local leaders and organizations from the cultural communities being served by T-CATs to help fund their operations. Churches, mosques, synagogues, immigrant ethnic associations, minority sport teams, or ethnic markets can be excellent sponsors for personnel or resources.

• Provide tax incentives and receipts, where possible, to donors of money or supplies from the public to a T-CAT.

Exercise:

Develop a model of funding to support a T-CAT in your agency or jurisdiction, based on the resources available.

1. Identify three sources of potential external funding in your local jurisdiction that you could approach to support T-CAT supplies and equipment in your agency.

2. Based on the size of your agency and its cross-cultural community needs, determine what the most appropriate services are that your T-CAT could provide to the community and agency, based on your available funding.

Photo TTP 2: Coordinating resources after Hurricane Ivan in Florida. (Photo by Andrea Booher/FEMA photo.)

TTP 3: CONDUCTING RAPID ASSESSMENTS AND LONG-RANGE PLANNING

Overview:

Many public safety and disaster response organizations in the United States and around the world are regularly challenged with identifying the different cultures within their jurisdictions; understanding the unique needs, attitudes, practices, and perceptions of these populations related to emergencies; and analyzing what the implications of these realities are for first responders serving these communities. As noted in the introductory chapters to this book, gaining and utilizing cultural knowledge about a population is a critically important but often overlooked tactical skill that can ultimately make a significant difference in the lives of civilians and the responders serving them in a crisis situation. To that end, one of the most important functions that a tactical anthropology team can provide to a public safety organization is the provision of knowledge about key elements of the culture of various populations within their area of operations. T-CATs can conduct rapid needs assessments, either as independent units or in conjunction with representatives from other agencies, and can gather important information that is essential for mission efforts, both when responding to immediate needs as well as planning for future operations. This information is critical for the agency in which the T-CAT is based, but is also important to partnering organizations. Rapid needs assessments are qualitative in nature; what they lack in size and precision, they make up for in nuanced depth of understanding about an issue. They do not require asking hundreds or even thousands of people about their opinions. Instead, rapid needs assessments are informal field ethnographic surveys that rely on a much smaller number of in-depth conversations with key individuals in a community in order to understand their issues and priorities.

Tactics, Techniques, and Procedures:

•Conduct rapid needs assessments among the subcultures within a jurisdiction as a tactical cultural asset team utilizing field ethnographic techniques. Repeat these needs assessments on a regular basis, potentially every other year or even more frequently, depending on mobility and turnover in a community.

•In most cases for T-CAT rapid emergency response planning, use general estimates, averages, and approximations for many key pieces of information that are needed planning and future operation purposes.

•Do not rely on just one source of information to gather a point of data. Cross check the findings by seeking the same kinds of information from multiple sources, either in-person or through written means.

•Develop trusting, warm, and caring relationships with key leaders and points of contact within diverse communities. These individuals can be ongoing sources of important information about their community, and are often willing to work as partners in gathering needs assessment information to address emergencies and disasters.

●Collect key community information on an ongoing basis, and compare it over time for trend lines. Assess these trends and analyze their implications for emergency response purposes. Are there new populations in the community who need interpretors? Has a new company opened up that recruits refugees?

●Utilize a variety of sources to understand community dynamics when conducting rapid needs assessments. Rely primarily on face-to-face conversations with key individuals, but supplement information as needed with written and other sources.

●Use a "snowball" effect for interviewing. Start the rapid needs assessment by meeting with the most logical sources of information within a community, such as tribal leaders or ethnic association representatives or heads of religious institutions. If they do not know the answers to your questions, ask them for referrals to other sources of information in the community that would know.

●Conduct on-site visits to communities and have first-hand conversations with residents from a variety of diverse perspectives. Visit with ethnic store owners, religious leaders, ethnic association representatives, schools, worksites, recreation teams, parents, elders, ethnic newspapers, ethnic radio stations, laundromats, food banks, clinics, and any other relevant venue. Ask respondents for other ideas about where else to go for further information.

•Allow adequate time to conduct a qualitative rapid needs assessment. This process may take several days to several weeks or months, but is nonetheless typically faster than a formal quantitative scientific study, which may take a year or more to finish and tends to have very low response rates within many culturally diverse communities due to language, culture, income, and literacy barriers. Many conversations with community members in a rapid assessment may take an hour or more, and should include time in the beginning for personal connections before proceeding to any business.

•Where possible, utilize the most culturally appropriate T-CAT members to conduct conversations with community members. For instance, in some cases, it may be best to have a female T-CAT staff meet with a local ethnic women's association, but an older male member could be sent to visit with clan elders that are men. Older T-CAT members of either gender are often most effective when working with many middle aged or senior members of these communities, while young T-CAT staff can often engage well with younger community members.

•Consider different mechanisms of face-to-face contact with community members in order to conduct a needs assessment related to emergency response topics. This could include, for instance, individual in-person conversations with key community members; on-site neighborhood visits to important venues; small group meetings; mid-size focus group sessions; or even large town hall gatherings to solicit information and input about emergency and disaster topics.

Situational Tactical Exercise:

Use the following table as a basic guide to plan how you would conduct a rapid needs assessment within your area of operations as a tactical cultural asset team member. Review the main points of information that should be gathered for emergency response and future operations planning. One of these forms should be completed for each main subpopulation in a community. Within each of these identified cultural communities in your jurisdiction, where could you find this information? What other questions would be important to explore in your communities that would be helpful to understand from an emergency response standpoint?

Tactical Situation Exercise

EMERGENCY PLANNING INFORMATION	RESPONSES AND/OR ESTIMATES
Name of Cultural Community	
Primary Languages Spoken	
Ethnic, Clan, or Tribal Subgroups	
General Level of Literacy in Host Language	
Preferred Methods for Receiving Emergency Information (radio stations, newspapers, websites, social media, in-person, faith meetings, etc.)	
Approximate Size of Population and Common Household Patterns (extended families, average household size, head of household, etc.)	
Key Anchor Employers (if any)	
Key Religious or Faith Institutions	
Key Schools or Colleges in Community	
Key Markets or Stores in the Community	
Key Ethnic Associations, Facebook Pages, Newspapers, and Community Leaders that Could Assist with Messaging and Emergencies	
Estimated Average Income Level of Families (very low, low, medium, or high compared to host population)	
General Modes of Transportation in Community	
General Level of Familiarity with Local Safety Protocols during Disasters (basements for tornadoes, etc.)	
Common Perceptions, Attitudes, or Practices that Could Affect Emergency Response and Planning	
General Ability to Recover after Disasters	
Special Cultural Prohibitions that Could Affect Emergency Planning (male and female segregation; special dietary needs, ethnic conflict with a neighboring population; etc.)	
Any Additional Points of Relevance	

Photo TTP 3: American Red Cross Rapid Health Assessment "Hot Shot" Teams gather for their morning briefing after Hurricane Harvey in Houston. (Photo by Mark Grey, with permission.)

TTP 4: UTILIZING CULTURAL INFORMATION TO UNDERSTAND POPULATIONS

Overview:

One of the most valuable skills that T-CAT members must learn is how to find and utilize socio-cultural intelligence to develop effective emergency response plans and operations for vulnerable communities in their jurisdiction. This is also among the most important assets that T-CATS can share with other agencies in order to ensure that first responders are fully knowledgeable about the needs and group characteristics of civilian populations with their area of operations. Sociocultural information or intelligence is essentially population-based information about communities. It is commonly referred to as demographic information, and is essential for planning and response purposes. Abbreviated as SOCINT, it is roughly equivalent to the kinds of information that defense strategists use to assess the "white layer" or civilian populations in their areas of operation. SOCINT should not be confused with HUMINT, which is human-based intelligence, usually collected from individual confidential sources and typically utilized to target criminals for arrest, as an example. SOCINT, on the other hand, refers to demographic information about a population, such as its estimated size, average income level, general literacy level, common family structures within that population, languages spoken, and other factors. Unfortunately, many public safety agencies have a poor history of understanding the populations in their jurisdictions, and do not routinely identify or assess open-source demographic characteristics of these groups through SOCINT. It is no wonder, then, that emergency response missions sometimes fail because responders are tactically proficient but have little understanding of the populations they are serving. Gathering SOCINT is not illegal, nor is it profiling. This kind of group-based demographic information is used regularly by government agencies, non-profits, city organizations, and other entities to manage their responses effectively and budget the appropriate resources to meet the needs of at-risk communities.

Tactics, Techniques, and Procedures:

●Regular assess demographic information on communities within your local area of operations. This information should be reviewed regularly, as it can change frequently and unexpectedly if populations are particularly mobile.

●Utilize open sources of information to better understand the special populations within a jurisdiction. The open sources of data are important supplements to face-to-face meetings with community members to better understand their needs. Some free, open-sources of information about specific populations can include google searches, facebook pages, ethnic association websites, community event postings, ethnic newspapers and journals, and other such sources.

●In the field, use computers, smartphones, tablets, or other devices as ethnographic, anthropologic tools that can provide instant information on a population with which a T-CAT may be working. For instance, in a crisis, if a T-CAT runs into a refugee population from an ethnic group they do not know, a quick google search about that population can often provide socio-cultural information such as migration history, traditional practices, and cultural patterns about this population from a national or global perspective.

• If resources allow in an agency, particularly if a T-CAT is serving a regional or larger area, consider purchasing subscriptions to professional cultural databases for use by responders. These databases often provide finger-tip access in the field or office to responders that have a sudden need for background information regarding a particular culture.

• Avoid relying on national or state census data for sociocultural intelligence to understand the many micro-populations that are often in a community. This is particularly true for many immigrant and refugee populations that are often undercounted in census studies due to their mobility, questionable legal status, language barriers, and other factors. The only way to fully understand these local diverse populations is to meet with them in person, conduct a rapid field needs assessment, and gather legal SOCINT from open sources about them so that their needs can be better met in emergencies.

• Ensure that group-based sociocultural information is not used for racial profiling purposes or stereotyping of individuals within a community. This group-based information simply provides general guidance on the commonalities and trends within a community for planning purposes, but should not be applied to an individual from that population.

Drill:

You are a T-CAT member assisting the state emergency management office in Michigan in the United States. A severe ice storm and blizzard is expected to hit the state tomorrow. The emergency management office has requested your assistance in providing weather information to the large population of Arab Americans in the state of Michigan and planning for possible sheltering if power goes out. In 15 minutes, find out everything you can using your telephone, laptop, tablet, or other handy source of information about this population and determine the following:

1. General size of this population in the state

2. Main geographic areas of concentration

3. Primary languages spoken and cultural groups represented

4. Potential community organizations or leaders that you might reach out to for assistance with emergency messaging, coalition partnering, etc.

5. Other important social, cultural, and economic information that would be helpful to know for disaster operations

Photo TTP 4: Meeting of newcomers from Palau to discuss available resources in Postville, Iowa after a large federal immigration action. (Photo by Mark Grey, with permission.)

TTP 5: ENGAGING KEY LEADERS IN CULTURAL COMMUNITIES

Overview:

The ability to identify key leaders in communities, engage with them effectively before, during, and after emergencies; and develop long-term trusting relationships with them is one of the most fundamental services that tactical cultural asset teams can provide for their organizations. All too often, this has been a topic that has been sorely overlooked by public safety and emergency response agencies. The need for information on local community leaders in diverse cultures is too often not considered in mission planning or emergency response operations, in part because many agencies have only limited understanding of the subcultures within their jurisdictions, or do not understand the leadership patterns within these populations. Some of the most common phrases heard during emergencies in public safety agencies as a crisis unfolds is: "Who are 'their' leaders? Where do 'they' live, and how can we reach 'them'?" Sadly, when emergency agencies have failed to engage local leaders in diverse communities as partners in planning for disasters and other crises, casualty rates among civilians can be disproportionately higher in these communities and response/recover operations can be unnecessarily complex, costly, and risky. Tactical Cultural Asset Teams must be thoroughly familiar with the major subpopulations within their jurisdictions and develop meaningful, trusting relationships with local leaders, tribal heads, clan elders, and other influential members of these communities in order to prepare for, respond to, and recover from disasters, civil unrest and other emergencies in the area of operations.

Tactics, Techniques, and Procedures:

• When conducting a rapid needs assessment in a community, identify not just the subpopulations that are present, but the key leaders, cultural brokers, and other individuals of influence within that group. These key leaders are typically informal sources of power and decision-making within a community, and are not necessarily elected officials.

• Engage with key community leaders ahead of time, prior to disaster response or emergency operations. Build long-term, trusting, face-to-face relationships with these key leaders and maintain them through regular meetings on-site in their communities and visits to their homes and neighborhoods. Invite them to also come to your agency and meet its leaders, as well as other members of your T-CAT. Ask for their opinions and value their viewpoints about how best to partner with them on emergency operations.

• Allow time to get know community leaders on a personal level, both during meetings as well as in a broader sense. Conducting meetings that are limited in time and get "straight down to business" can often seem rude and impersonal to many immigrants and refugees. Allow key leaders to share their stories, experiences, and concerns, even if this means you must have multiple meetings before ultimately discussing partnership opportunities.

• Utilize interpreters when needed at any key leader engagements, and understand the appropriate cultural communication style that is common in that population. Honor those leaders.

●Recognize that key leaders can change often due to migration, political infighting, demographic shifts, and other factors. T-CATS should maintain a current roster of key leaders in local cultural communities, and ensure that this roster is up-to-date by attending periodic face-to-face meetings with these leaders to ensure that their influence within a population is still valid.

●Utilize various methods to identify key informal leaders in cultural communities. This can range from having multiple conversations with community members and asking for their opinions and recommendations, as well as conducting open-source reviews of socio-cultural information, such as internet and Facebook searches for leaders of various ethnic communities within the T-CAT's jurisdiction.

●Because many immigrants have extended family networks and close ties with one another, contact ethnic leaders in larger urban areas to see if they have referrals to local leaders in small communities nearby.

●Be sure to recognize the subtle diversity-within-diversity possibilities when trying to identify key leaders. For instance, identifying a single "Sudanese" community leader would often be difficult, because ethnic identity in this population is often split between northern and southern Sudan, Christian vs. Muslim, and tribal affiliations. This would also apply for many other cultures where language, religion, nation of origin, family history, tribe, and clan can be extremely important to know and understand, and identifying a single community leader to represent this level of diversity within one group would be extremely difficult.

•Interview ethnic market and restaurant owners, faith leaders, employers, teachers, landlords and other key sectors of the community in order to gauge public opinion and help identify local leaders.

•Consider gender and age factors when identifying community partners and key leaders. For instance, in some cultures, men play a more powerful than women in representing their families to the public, and so are often main points of contact. In other cultures, though, women have an extremely powerful role both at home and in the community, and can be extremely important key leaders. Likewise, age is important in many traditional cultures, and older people are often considered to be representatives and natural leaders within their clans, tribes, and communities than younger people would be. By conducting a simple internet search on "common family structure and practices" within a certain population, important social and cultural information can be gained quickly that can provide a T-CAT with ideas about these cultural norms.

•In the field, utilize smart phones like portable ethnographic computer databases. When in doubt, literally conduct an internet search with key words such as "ethnic association of (group) in (region), and see what comes up from that search. Often community leader information can be gathered by contacting local ethnic associations and asking for referrals about leaders in a local region.

● Triangulate all information gathered about recommendations for key community leaders, and vet these persons among other subpopulations. Be sure to ask the opinions of both men and women, old and young, and various ethnic sub-groups in order to get a better feel for how well certain people might be perceived as key leaders in their community.

Drill:

You have training in tactical anthropology from your home public safety agency, but are visiting your public health friends in Waterloo, Iowa in the United States for vacation. On television, there is a report that a growing outbreak of the deadly Ebola virus in Western Africa could potentially affect Liberian refugees in Midwestern states due to frequent travel of relatives between both nations. Your friends turn to you for rapid advice on how to find community leaders within the Liberian population in their state and local city, so that they can begin discussing emergency communications and messaging about preventing this disease.

1. Conduct a rapid internet search to identify some points of contact from the Liberian refugee community in Iowa.

2. Who would be some of the Liberian refugee referrals that you would make to your public health friends as starting points to identify community leaders in this population in Iowa, the Midwest, and the United States?

Photo TTP 5: African American Leadership Summit in Washington, D.C. (Photo by Taneska Hankerson/FEMA photo.)

TTP 6: SERVING VULNERABLE POPULATIONS THROUGH COALITIONS

Overview:

Tactical anthropology team members should spend much of their time engaging with key leaders from specific cultural communities at the local field level, as described in the previous chapter. However, in order to be most effective in preparing communities to survive disasters and recover from large scale emergencies that affect wide areas, T-CATs can serve as agents of change in their surrounding regions, states, or joint jurisdictions by developing or participating in strong coalitions of multiple cultural groups and specialists to address these challenges at higher levels. These cultural coalitions, which can be lead, organized, or joined by T-CAT members, essentially function at the operational and/or strategic levels, rather than the tactical field levels. These higher-level coalitions focus on preparing communities socially to withstand mass chaotic events and recover from these emergency situations more effectively as a region than what can be done at the individual household level in the field. Participation and engagement of T-CAT members on regional boards, state councils, tri-state emergency response task forces, and other such entities can provide often overlooked information on the needs of culturally diverse and economically underserved communities in these larger areas of operations. Many regional emergency response and disaster preparedness coalitions have little understanding of the needs of special populations or minority communities within their large area of operations, and could greatly benefit from the expertise of T-CAT representatives in these groups.

Tactics, Techniques, and Procedures:

•Seek opportunities as T-CAT members to serve on regional, tri-state, or other large jurisdiction coalitions, task forces, advisory boards, councils, and related entities that address topics such as emergency preparedness, disaster response, and homeland security planning.

•Provide information to these organizations on the variety of cultural communities within their jurisdiction, the approximate size of these populations, languages spoken, estimated literacy and income levels, and other important considerations for emergency preparation, response, and recovery.

•Assist representatives from other areas in the coalition in identifying key cultural leaders within their communities and conducting needs assessments with these groups to improve disaster planning and response.

•Provide guidance to the coalition on unintended second and third order effects that could happen if the needs of vulnerable populations are not considered in emergency response and planning, such as more casualties and hgher costs.

•Encourage the coalition in reaching out to key leaders or representatives from cultural communities within their region to serve also on these task forces or planning committees. If these representatives cannot attend meetings regularly in person, provide alternative methods of participation, such as facetime, skype, google hangouts, or conference calls. If they still cannot participate, consider bringing ideas directly to these key leaders on-site where they live or work, in order to ask their opinions about emergency response and planning.

●Help the coalition in developing and maintaining an emergency roster of key community leaders and important organizations within vulnerable populations of the region, as well as a set of referrals and resources for these groups. Many of these populations are interconnected and/or related, so resources can often be shared if culturally appropriate.

●Partner with and advocate for the needs of special populations in emergencies within these larger jurisdictions. The needs of these groups often goes overlooked, as coalitions address areas of operation that expand in scope.

Case Study:

Within your own community, identify task forces, coalitions, or other collaborative entities that function at regional or larger levels that are relevant for your agency in addressing emergency response or homeland security issues. How familiar do you think these groups are with the cultural diversity within your jurisdiction? How could a tactical anthropologist be of use to these groups?

Photo TTP 6: Tribal Relations Summit in Placerville, California. (Photo by Adam DuBrowa/FEMA photo.)

TTP 7: CONDUCTING CROSS-CULTURAL OUTREACH AND EDUCATION

Overview:

One of the most important responsibilities that a tactical cultural asset team should be responsible for in a first response agency or regional coalition is providing direct education and outreach services on disaster awareness, emergency response protocols, legal guidelines for safe practices, and related topics. If the T-CAT does not have the resources to provide this education directly through community policing, neighborhood forums, or other such public engagement opportunities, the team should at least be able to help coordinate such programs or make referrals for community leaders needing education on these topics. Equally important is recognizing that much of this education and outreach should be done before, rather than during or after, a civil crisis or emergency response. Many agencies spend too much money and resources responding to emergencies that could have been mitigated or prevented through pre-planning and effective cross-cultural community engagement before a need occurs. Today, this need for front-end tactical education and outreach is even more critical in the culturally complex areas of operations that make up many urban areas in the United States and other nations. First response agencies are not always familiar with the level of cultural and linguistic diversity in their jurisdictions, and do not understand the need to reach out to these communities before a crisis or disaster occurs. Emergency management personnel that refuse to recognize the level of diversity in their communities will often pay a high price in unnecessary response costs, greater risk to their responders and even higher civilian casualties after a large scale crisis. Strong community relationships with the local T-CAT should be developed ahead of time, and educational outreach programs are some of the best engagement opportunities to do so with the public.

Tactics, Techniques, and Procedures:

●Conduct or coordinate cross-cultural community education and outreach activities on emergencies after a rapid needs assessment has been finished in the area of operations and key cultural communities have been identified.

●Provide culturally appropriate education and outreach activities before a crisis or large scale emergency occurs, rather than during or after, for greatest impact. Outreach activities that occur too late in the emergency response cycle may be completely worthless, or may only mitigate, rather than prevent, casualties among civilians and responders alike.

●Develop trust with the target communities before, during, and after education and outreach activities. Remember that many immigrant and refugee populations in an area of operations may be new to a community, unfamiliar with its resources or safety concerns, and may not have ever been exposed to police, fire, military, or other kinds of public safety personnel back home. If they were, these entities may have been corrupt or dangerous to the public, and were typically not trusted. Spend time to educate new immigrants about public safety professionals and emergency responders in the host community where these new residents now live.

●Consider conducting training and outreach activities on some of the most important topics for communities, especially those comprised of newer immigrants. Such training topics could include the proper use of 911 emergency assistance; safety during hurricanes, tornadoes, floods, and other such disasters; fire prevention; family evacuation and reunification plans; and other topics of interest to a particular community itself.

●Provide culturally specific outreach programs when budget and resources allow, rather than in a mixed cultural forum. This allows the T-CAT to better address the perceptions, attitudes, and knowledge levels about a particular public safety topic through culturally specific programming.

●Utilize verbal or face-to-face gatherings when conducting education and outreach. Small group settings are best, but larger community gatherings can also be effective. Communicating through websites, posters, and other written mechanisms is much less effective with almost all these populations.

●Carefully consider the most appropriate venue for conducting disaster and emergency education programs in cultural communities. Many families face significant transportation and financial barriers to services, so outreach programs are best conducted on-site, where individuals live, work, play, study, shop, or worship. Many excellent trainings have been conducted with community members, for instance, at the anchor employers where large numbers of immigrants may be at a worksite during lunch, or even after a church service for a specific ethnic population.

•Do not expect large numbers of community members to come to your organization for a talk on emergency preparedness. Go to the community instead at times likely to have greater attendance, such as evenings or weekends.

•Look for "windows of opportunity" where large numbers of a target population already is gathered, such as at an ethnic soccer tournament, rather than creating a separate outreach event, in order to set up community outreach and education.

•Utilize ethnic store owners, religious leaders, sports teams, women's groups, ethnic associations, and other such entities of important within a cultural community as partners in sponsoring educational activities or sharing messaging to their public.

•When possible, conduct public safety education and outreach in the native language of the target population. Identify interpreters ahead of time, and allow for outreach activities that will take approximately two-to-three times as long as they would if no interpretation was needed. Community leaders can also help identify interpreters to assist with these activities.

Scenario:

The jurisdiction of a particular public safety agency in a small urban area with 50,000 people in the United States has a large white and African American population. However, it recently has had new influxes of refugees from Burma (Southeast Asia) and the Democractic Republic of the Congo (Central Africa) who are working in the local meatpacking plant. Most of the Burmese have never finished second grade, because they lived in refugee camps. However, many of the Congolese were teachers and nurses back home. Most are not literate in English among either immigrant group. Major flooding is expected in the next four days along the river in the community where everyone now lives.

1. What strategies would you utilize to conduct outreach and education on flood safety with these four populations BEFORE a disaster would ever hit?

2. If you were on a T-CAT, what agencies, organizations, or other ethnic entities might you reach out to as partners in flood evacuation outreach for each of these groups?

Photo TTP 7: Interviewing a refugee from Burma for a search and rescue exercise in Iowa. (Photo by Mark Grey, with permission.)

TTP 8: COMMUNICATING CROSS-CULTURALLY DURING EMERGENICES

Overview:

In times of mass emergencies, social crisis, and disasters, accurate information can save lives, reduce the costs of response and recovery, and minimize risk to first responders. However, providing effective, accurate, and meaningful information to the public that results in the desired outcomes from a safety standpoint can be challenging at best, and particularly difficult when working cross-culturally with language and literacy barriers among immigrant, refugee, and other special populations. Communities that are comprised of "super diversity" or even "micro diversity", as discussed in the introductory section of this book, can present especially difficult situations for public safety agencies from a crisis communications standpoint. Tactical cultural asset teams can and should play an important role in helping disseminate important community messaging with public information officers (PIOs) by identifying cultural communities that may need special communications strategies; helping develop these messages; and ultimately providing guidance and/or leadership in disseminating this information to the public. Too often during emergencies, public information offices provide guidance to the public, but do not necessarily consider the special needs of vulnerable populations such as immigrants, refugees, low-income families, and others that have unique language, literacy, cultural, and economic barriers that can affect their ability to access or understand this information. T-CATs can help mitigate some of these challenges.

Tactics, Techniques, and Procedures:

●Hold planning meetings with the public information office of their agency or other appropriate entities prior to emergencies or disasters in their jurisdictions in order to develop a cross-cultural crisis communications plan.

●Provide socio-cultural information and demographic insights to public information officers regarding the level of diversity within their area of operations; approximate size of these populations; languages spoken; estimated literacy levels; preferred modes of communication; and other key factors.

●Meet with key leaders in cultural communities prior to disasters and other mass emergencies occurring. Do not wait for these chaotic events to happen before deciding how to communicate safety information about them.

●Based on meetings with key community leaders, develop an action plan for crisis communication. With input from the community, decide what modes of communication are most effective for them. These could include television, radio, ethnic association Facebook pages, in-person emergency forums led by religious leaders, telephone text alerts, etc.

●In some cases, particularly if an emergency is already happening, combine mass communication strategies with in-person, door-to-door messaging through home visits, utilization of megaphones from the back of a pickup truck for mandatory evacuations, or other field strategies that connect personally with individuals.

●Consider age, gender, and other factors that could influence the way emergency messaging should be shared with a community. For instance, although Facebook posts may be fast and helpful for young bilingual members of a cultural community, they are often of little use to elders or older audiences that do not use social media and are in positions of power in their communities.

●Because gender roles in culture can be important for community messaging and decision making, target emergency information appropriately. If working in a face-to-face venue, it can also be helpful to have female T-CAT members meet with women in traditionally conservative communities, while male members visit with the men in the community.

●Where possible as a T-CAT, provide emergency messaging through face-to-face venues, either with individuals from a community, or through small forums or larger group sessions. Allow at least double the time for interpretation if needed. This is particularly important when working with low-literacy populations.

●Utilize the appropriate cultural communication style as needed when conducting emergency messaging, especially through in-person venues. As discussed in the introductory section of this book, some cultures are more direct and expressive, while others value restraint and understatement. Ask for guidance from local community members about how best to present information that may be very graphic and disturbing.

Exercise:

Your T-CAT has been asked to provide guidance to the local County Emergency Management Agency on developing a strategic plan for dissemination of emergency disaster response information for the three main cultural populations in the community. For each of the groups below, what recommendations would you make about how best to communicate with these groups during a crisis?

1. White population; 30,000 persons; lower to middle class; miscellaneous blue collar workers; some homeless and/or unemployed

2. African American upper class population; 500 persons (primarily faculty, staff, students, and families associated with the local Historically Black College and University in the community); 1,000 persons

3. New Karenni refugee population; 2,000 persons; very low literacy in native language; primarily working in several large agricultural processing facilities in town; tend to live together in a number of apartment buildings

Photo TTP 8: FEMA meeting with the Muslim Community in Brighton Beach, New York after Hurricane Sandy. (Photo by Ashley Andujar/FEMA photo.)

TTP 9: WORKING WITH LOW-INCOME COMMUNITIES

Overview:

Many immigrant, refugee, and ethnic minority communities are more likely to be affected by disasters and related emergencies, as well as have higher injury and accident rates, than many majority populations in host communities around the world. While language and cultural barriers can certainly contribute to these disparities in outcomes, one of the most common unifying factors affecting many of these diverse populations is poverty. Populations in poorer communities, regardless of their culture or ethnicity, tend to have higher morbidity and mortality rates, and are disproportionately likely to be affected by hurricanes, floods, tornadoes, civil unrest, and other mass emergency situations. For instance, in the United States, emergency planners are well aware that families in trailer parks are at particular risk for injury or death during tornadoes, regardless of their racial background. Similarly, immigrant and refugee populations that may live in tightly packed and overcrowded apartment buildings owned by landlords that may turn a blind eye to safety code violations, can be particularly at risk for building fires and the spread of infectious diseases.

For tactical anthropology teams, one of the most important predictors that should be used for emergency response planning and recovery purposes is an estimate of the average income level of the populations they are serving. If they are working with lower income families in certain neighborhoods, T-CATs should anticipate that these families may experience a number of heightened challenges before, during, and after an emergency, regardless of their race or ethnicity. Many of these populations do actually work, but may be employed with companies that they pay them little and offer few benefits. Some of the challenges that are linked to low income and socioeconomic levels include transportation barriers to evacuation; childcare barriers to attending distant community meetings on disaster preparedness; double shift employment hours that make it difficult to seek relief supplies after a crisis; and many others. Many lower income populations are less likely to be prepared for a disaster; will be the most vulnerable during the crisis; and are the slowest to recover from the mass emergency. Working with lower income populations is increasingly a skill that T-CATs must master and teach to their colleagues.

Tactics, Techniques, and Procedures:

●Assess the general income level of the key populations being served in the community by the first response agency. Be familiar with any key anchor companies that employ many of the residents in their communities, and knowledgeable of the kinds of shifts and days with which these populations work. T-CATS should also know if most of the populations are working legally or are undocumented in their community, as well as what kinds of insurance they may have, as this information can affect many issues, including trust of providers, resources available, and opportunities for emergency messaging.

•Where possible, in order to minimize travel, childcare, geographical, and other income-related barriers to services, hold public safety meetings and information sessions on-site, where families live, work, study, play, shop, or worship. Leaders of these venues can be valuable in helping T-CATs set up these face-to-face sessions before, during, and after emergencies.

•Recognize the strong link between income and education. Communities that are lower income will typically require programming and emergency services that are geared towards populations with lower literacy levels, which is explained further in the next chapter. Programming is usually best done with these populations through T-CAT engagements that are in person and built on trust.

•Provide emergency and disaster services at times and on days that are convenient for the population that is affected, particularly for those that are lower income. For instance, in immigrant neighborhoods where most of the adults are working at a local anchor company like a warehouse for six days a week, double shift, will have difficulty coming to a relief office that is only open Monday through Friday, from 9:00 am to 5:00 pm. Alternative services could be provided during evenings and late nights, and/or on weekends, in order to meet their needs. Alternatively, the anchor company could host disaster assistance programmers over lunch on site at their place of employment.

•Allow for greater time when conducting visits with families that are lower income. They often will have a number of barriers and challenges affecting their well-being before, during, and after an emergency that must be addressed during these sessions. Meetings and interaction with them can often take longer than with populations that may be higher income or have more resources to help them.

•Build trusting relationships between T-CAT members and local families in lower income areas. Be willing to provide resources, referrals, and points of contact to these families on issues that may not be specifically related to emergency services, as they often ask for this assistance when trust has been built.

Case Study:

During Typhoon Yolanda in the Philippines in 2013, more than 6,300 people died. Many of these victims lived in low-lying coastal areas, flood plains, and river banks in shantytowns and squatter settlements.

1. How do you think poverty played a role in contributing to these deaths?

2. If you were on a tactical anthropology team in an international disaster relief agency, what advice would you give to these communities regarding rebuilding and recovery?

3. If they are too poor to move to higher ground in richer areas, what would be their alternatives?

Photo TTP 9: Signing up disaster survivors for low-interest loans. (Photo by Marilee Callendo/FEMA photo.)

TTP 10: WORKING WITH LOW-LITERACY FAMILIES

Overview:

One of the most common challenges faced by first responders, but arguably one of the least understood, is the general level of literacy and education among the populations they serve in the area of operations. Many public safety professionals wrongly assume that the civilians in their communities are well educated, literate, and able to easily understand emergency response information and messaging that is provided them through websites, flyers, Facebook postings, and other forms of written communication. In reality, though, literacy levels are often much lower than responders assume, and public safety messaging can easily be misunderstood or misinterpreted, as it is often incorrectly written at high school or college levels. This can be particularly unfortunate when it leads to unnecessary levels of chaos and casualties during an actual emergency. For instance, during the mega-hurricane Yolanda that occurred in 2013 in the Philippines, some emergency response agencies used the technically accurate term "potential storm surge" in their evacuation warning messages to the public. After more than 6,300 residents drowned or otherwise died in this mass disaster, many survivors complained afterwards that they did not understand the meteorologically correct phrase "storm surge", and they were angry that the messaging did not use the simpler term "tidal wave" so that their families would have know to evacuate to much higher ground.

In many cases, more than 50% of a population, even with residents that are educated, may have functional literacy challenges. When working with lower income or immigrant populations, potentially 80% or more may not be able to comprehend written information well enough. To that end, Tactical Cultural Asset Teams must assess the general literacy level of the subcultures that it serves, and ensure that communication before, during, and after a crisis is at the appropriate level for the greatest comprehension by the public.

Tactics, Techniques, and Procedures:

●Recognize that literacy challenges can exist even in majority populations in host communities, let alone among new immigrants and refugees in those areas of operations.

●For any written material produced, aim for approximately a fifth or sixth grade level for host populations. When working with immigrant populations, this may need to be as low as second or third grade.

●Pilot test any written material produced, distributed, or utilized by the T-CAT for comprehension by a target population. Just because a family can read, does not mean that they can correctly comprehend the information being shared in writing.

●When sharing written information with the public on emergencies and disasters, ensure that the words used in the material is simple and easy to understand. The public is not impressed with big, complicated words, but rather can be confused by them. Make sure that paragraphs are short, and sentences do not run on in length. Use bullet points to get main messages across, instead of long narratives.

●Use websites and other tools to review text that is written for the public, in order to estimate the grade level that it is targeting. A higher level of comprehension can be achieved by using simpler words, shorter sentences, fewer paragraphs, and words with fewer syllables.

●When developing written emergency material, make sure that only a few main points of information are shared. The human brain will remember these main points better if they are repeated several times in different ways.

●Do not overly rely on written materials for emergency communication and disaster education. When possible, this information will be best presented verbally to community forums, small groups, or key leaders for sharing with the broader public audience.

●Avoid causing embarrassment or negative social stigma to populations or families that may have low literacy. For instance, the case work chart of a family or individual with low literacy could be marked in a subtle way with a colored sticker inside of it, in order to let fellow disaster response staff know that this family needs more face-to-face and verbal help with understanding information.

•Utilize culturally appropriate visuals when possible to enhance written messages. However, be sure to pilot test these visuals for comprehension by the target audience so that they are not misunderstood or offensive. For instance, photographs of people should look like the target civilian population, rather than another major ethnic group.

•Recognize that populations can also have issues understanding and interpreting visuals, which is a form of symbolic literacy. Many symbols, such as a red cross, are culturally specific for instance, and may not identify the location of a first aid kit. Use visuals and symbols that are understood by the target cultural population, and meaningful for them.

•Allow for extra time by public safety professionals to verbally explain numeric information, in addition to any written instructions given to the public. Civilians and other members of the public often struggle even more with numeric literacy, or the understand of math and formulas in written messages. For instance, a physician assistant who is responding to a disaster recovery operation, may have difficulty explaining a prescription to a patient that she must take 2 tablets, four times a day, for the next 10 days, before cutting the dosage in half.

Table Top Exercise:

Consider your agency's area of operations. Within your jurisdiction, identify the following:

1.What neighborhoods or populations are most likely to have lower levels of literacy and education?

2.What methods of education are your agency currently using to reach these populations before, during, and after an emergency amd how can T-CAT be useful in developing or identifying information programs for lower literacy populations?

Photo TTP 10: Providing guidance to survivors of Hurricane Maria in Puerto Rico. (Photo Eduardo Martinez/FEMA photo.)

TTP 11: WORKING WITH GENDER, AGE AND RELIGIOUS DIFFERENCES

Overview:

Emergency response and disaster relief professionals must have excellent skills in working with families during times of crisis. For instance, globally, approximately 80% of refugees are estimated to be mothers and children. In other emergencies, parents may be injured or killed, children can be separated from their caretakers, families may feel hopeless, emotions can be stretched to levels never before experienced, and decision makers may not know how best to lead their families through times of severe human stress. These normal reactions to the abnormal circumstances of being involved in a major emergency or disaster can be exacerbated by differences in cultural and religious roles, or the traditional views that an ethnic community may have about men and women, and the old and young. First responders and emergency personnel typically have not considered the implications of different social roles roles within the populations they may be serving in culturally diverse communities. For instance, emergency messaging may be published by a county response agency in English on a Facebook page that might reach young people, but not in the second language spoken by the elder tribal leaders in a particular refugee community that could be influential in leading their community to make evacuation decisions. In another situation, the civilian population affected by a large hurricane could be comprised of Orthodox Jews or East African Muslims, who would likely not be able to consume the large number of pork sandwiches being donated by a local relief agency for dinner in a shelter, due to their religious prohibitions. As many first responders too often focus on the act of response, rather than the culture of the people being rescued and the complex social relationships in their families, mission operations can sometimes be unnecessarily challenging and difficult. They can also be costly in both economic and human terms for both the civilians and the emergency professionals serving them. Tactical Anthropology teams can play an important role for their agencies or jurisdictions by fully assessing the age and gender structure within the different cultural communities they are serving; understanding how the traditional age and gender roles within these cultures can affect response operations; and then training their fellow law enforcement, medical, fire, or other emergency management personnel in how best to modify their missions and planning to meet the special needs of these populations in a timely and effective manner.

Tactics, Techniques, and Procedures:

●For response planning purposes, determine the common family structure within the cultural community that is being served. Is it typically a small nuclear family made up of parents and a few children, or do they live together in large extended families? Consider the implications of these family structures for estimating the likely number of people that might be living in a home, neighborhood, or apartment building affected by an emergency.

●Determine the religion of the cultural populations that are being served. Many immigrant and refugee populations are quite religious, and their faith leaders can serve as powerful collaborators with emergency responders during a crisis.

●Identify and utilize local faith leaders that are in influential in a cultural community as partners in emergency planning, response, and recovery. These leaders can assist in sharing emergency information with their communities; usually know the deeper family relationships and politics between individuals; can serve as informal chaplains; and will often be helpful in providing mental health comfort to the community in times of crisis.

●Remember that religion comes out of culture, and is an integral part of ethnic identity for many people. Understand and learn about the religious beliefs, practices, and traditions of the population being served, so that these considerations can be incorporated into disaster planning and response

●Understand the traditional role of decision makers and gatekeepers by gender within the different cultural communities that are being served for planning and response purposes. Culturally, are men usually the representatives of the family to the public, or are women? Do women make the bulk of the decisions about the welfare of the family behind the scenes, or do they defer to the men? How does this affect mission planning or response operations? If men are expected to be the decision makers culturally, will they still share the needs and opinions of the mothers and wives in the community to the responders?

•Recognize the role that age plays in the culture of the population being served. In many traditional societies, great deference and respect is given to people that are older. If that is the case, include seniors and older members of the population in disaster and emergency planning and response to assist with decision making.

•If age is valued in a society, try to the limit the extent to which a first response agency is using young interpreters to work with older community leaders. Likewise, elders within the culture should be those selected to meet with police chiefs, fire captains, emergency managers, and other leaders during planning, response, and recovery meetings.

•Ensure that disaster or other relief operations consider gender, age, and religion in sheltering activities. For instance, some cultures typically separate men and women for religious and modesty purposes, so mixed-gender shelters would not be appropriate for these cultures. Showering, sleeping, eating, and recreational activities may need to be in separate areas for men and women in more conservative Muslim, Amish, orthodox Jewish, and other sects.

•Be certain to be familiar with typical cultural food practices and dietary patterns. For instance, orthodox Jews and religious Muslims will typically only eat food that is kosher or halal, and requires special consideration in sheltering operations. Pork is often considered "unclean" in a number of religions, and may not be the best choice when feeding large numbers of people from multiple unknown cultures. Local religious leaders can typically help T-CATs identify appropriate sources of culturally acceptable food.

•Where resources allow, match female T-CAT members with female community leaders, and male T-CAT members with male leaders in the cultural groups. While not politically correct" in some western cultures, this can be quite "culturally correct" in many traditional societies and more likely to produce improved levels of trust and engagement with local immigrant and refugee populations.

Table Top Exercise:

Your T-CAT has been asked to provide guidance on how to shelter up to 10,000 people from the local community that will be displaced by a severe flood in the next three days. There is a local school, community center, and empty warehouse in the town that have offered to provide shelter space to the evacuees.

1. How would the T-CAT recommend to the county emergency manager that these following groups be sheltered that live in the community?
   •8,000 local white residents;
   •800 Bosnian refugees who have lived there for 5 years;
   •200 Amish from nearby farms;
   •1,000 local Hispanics, some of whom are new migrant field workers and not well known to emergency responders.

2. What other special considerations exist for each of these groups from an age, gender, and religious standpoint that your T-CAT would want to make sure that emergency planners consider in response and recovery?

Photo TTP 11: Children playing in a Syrian refugee camp in Turkey. (Photo by Mark Grey, with permission.)

TTP 12: UNDERSTANDING LEGAL STATUS ISSUES

Overview:

One of the challenges for members of public safety agencies to understand is the great variety of legal status options which might exist among immigrant and refugee populations in their jurisdictions. Understanding the particular legal status which might be common in a particular community goes far beyond just meeting the common curiosity that a public safety provide may have as to why a certain population is residing in their jurisdiction. Understanding the legal status of individuals within these populations is actually critical to effective cross-cultural operations. Knowing this information can actually provide valuable information, for instance, about what resources and referrals might be available to victims and families after disasters; can help explain why a certain population may reside in a particular area; may help predict the kinds of emergencies and crime patterns that could occur in that group, and can often determine the level to which a certain community may be willing to partner with public safety organizations on emergency and disaster mitigation activities. Public safety providers must have a basic understanding of the different kinds of legal status that can be common among populations in their jurisdictions, in order to conduct effective strategic planning for future needs and operate successful missions in culturally complex communities. Members of Tactical Cultural Asset Teams should be familiar with these basic legal categories so that they can be shared with the broader public safety community, along with understanding the implications of emergency operations within populations from these different sectors of society.

Tactics, Techniques, and Procedures:

●Include questions that relate to understanding the legal status of families within a particular cultural population when conducting rapid needs assessments. It is not enough to know only the languages spoken or the ethnicities of those groups.

●Recognize that those populations with "refugee status" have most of the same rights and privileges of citizens in most countries. They cannot just be a refugee because they call themselves that. Under international definitions from the United Nations, refugees have been forced to flee their homes against their will due to a well-founded fear of death or persecution, and have crossed their own international border. Many reside initially in a neighboring country in a temporary camp or community, before a small number may ultimately be granted asylum in a third country like the United States, Germany, Canada, Sweden, Australia, and many others. In the United States, for instance, refugees are also typically entitled to many of the emergency response and disaster relief benefits and resources that local residents would have, as they are generally Permanent Residents or full citizens.

●By definition, many refugees would prefer to be back home, and thus often have higher rates of depression, anxiety, suicide, and post-traumatic stress than a host population. Understand that emergencies and disasters can exacerbate these feelings, particularly if language barriers exist. Many have witnessed or experienced war and genocide, and can be further traumatized during civil unrest.

•Recognize that refugee populations residing legally in communities will usually be comprised of larger family numbers, and often live in extended groups with each other in well-defined neighborhoods, apartment buildings, mobile home parks, and other such settings. It can sometimes be difficult to define households due to the fluid, large nature of extended families. However, these large families can serve as supports to victims and as partners with first responders during times of crisis.

•Understand that economic migrants are different from refugees, and may be in a nation either legally or illegally without the proper documentation. Economic migrants generally come to the United States and other host nations voluntarily in order to improve their lives and well-being. Some of these economic migrants have legal status to be a country, such as those on H1B visas in the United States that are foreign born physicians and engineers.

•Consider the planning and response implications for economic migrants that may be in a jurisdiction without the proper legal status, such as some migrant indigenous workers from Central America. These groups can be difficult to identify for planning purposes. They are sometimes the victims of human trafficking, both sex and labor, and often very reluctant to work together with law enforcement and other first responders. They may reside in "underground" housing units, such as in basements, large groups in one apartment, or in a room in a restaurant. They also disproportionately work in dangerous, black market jobs that make them highly susceptible to occupational injuries and accidents. Language and cultural barriers can be significant.

•Understand that undocumented economic migrants that are working in a country illegally may have almost no benefits, resources, or other supports before, during, and after disasters and public safety emergencies. Usually, only certain non-profit organizations, some religious groups, and perhaps local volunteers might be willing or able to provide these people with mental health counseling, case work, and other such needs after a crisis, but these organizations may not have the language or cultural resources to meet their needs effectively.

•Explore the level to which different international student populations reside in areas of operation, and become familiar with demographic information related to their groups in college towns. Due to funding cuts in many states, universities are increasingly recruiting international students to attend their institutions, as they pay much higher out-of-state tuition. In many college towns, residents can come from 30-50 different nationalities, with many living in small groups in certain areas off campus. The schools themselves can sometimes provide assistance with language interpretation and emergency messaging, as well as opportunities for first responders to present to these international students on disaster safety and related topics. These students are typically on J-1 visas, and generally return to their home countries upon completion of their studies.

•Become familiar with any populations in the community that may come from more unusual legal status categories and understand the implications of that for disaster and emergency services. For instance, many rural states like as Iowa in the United States are now recruiting workers from remote former territories, such as the Marshall Islands and

Micronesia, as meatpacking and other agricultural processing employees. That is because these populations, by treaty, can work legally in the United States. However, many are coming from nations with rare languages, unique cultures, and different beliefs and knowledge levels about public safety and emergency response topics. They may not be familiar with tornado safety, for example, or may not be prepared for severely frigid climates in winter that can cause hypothermia and death if stranded outside. Also, resource and referral agencies after disasters are not always familiar with these populations and sometimes do not even know if their agencies can provide them with recovery or other forms of assistance.

●Develop good relationships with local legal resources and immigration attorneys. T-CATs can turn to these specialists to answer legal questions related to the typical status that may be common in a particular population in a community, which can be helpful for planning purposes in emergency response.

●Understand that immigrant and refugee family members may have "mixed status." In other words, one person may be legally present in the community as a recognized refugee, but perhaps a brother has come to visit from a home nation and overstayed his tourist visa, so he is not residing legally in the area. Multiple kinds of legal status categories can exist in any one family on occasion, making the provision of emergency referrals and resources sometimes challenging.

Table Top Exercise:

You are part of an on-call Tactical Cultural Asset Team in a police department. A very strong hurricane is expected to hit your jurisdiction within the next three days. You have two unique cultural populations in your community on different kinds of legal status. One population is a group of refugees from Somalia in East Africa. They have been in your community for approximately ten years, and many own local businesses and restaurants in their ethnic neighborhood. The other population is a new group of migrant workers in your community, which you believe may be indigenous natives from Honduras. You have heard rumors that they work on the black market in local dairy operations, and have a low level of literacy even in their native language, and do not speak English. The United States has not granted refugee status to these migrants from Honduras, so you think that they are probably here working illegally and may even be victims of labor trafficking.

1. How would your emergency messaging differ for each population?

2. How might your evacuation plans and sheltering needs differ for each of these?

3. What resources and recovery services might your T-CAT recommend for each population?

Photo TTP 12: U.S. Citizenship and Immigration Services outreach in Orange County, California. (Photo by Cesar Baldemor/USCIS photo.)

TTP 13: WORKING WITH INTERPRETERS

Overview:

The ability to communicate effectively with the public during emergencies, disasters, and public safety crises is arguably the single most important consideration when conducting tactical anthropology operations. Interpretation refers to the conversion of spoken information, and translation refers to the conversion of written information. The lack of communication and miscommunication before, during, and after emergencies both verbally and in writing can contribute to higher injury and death rates among the public; unnecessary risk to responders; higher costs of operations; and slower community recovery. Today in the United States, though, as well as in numerous countries around the world, the number of languages and distinct dialects has proliferated, and even basic communication can be hampered. For instance, the United States Census (2015) estimates that over 380 languages are spoken in the nation today, and even small rural states like Iowa can boast more than 180 different languages due to the influx of refugee workers in key sectors of the economy.

In addition to the sheer diversity of common foreign languages currently spoken in many communities, responders are challenged to also meet the emergency needs of populations that speak languages that are linguistically classified as rare. These less common languages can be found among many indigenous families of Central American migrants, small tribal groups of African refugees, some Pacific Islander migrants, and other less common populations. For these individuals, it is sometimes impossible to find interpreters of any sort, including in-person or telephonic. To compound this challenge, some populations speak languages that have no written form, or they may not be literate in their own language, let alone that of the broader community.

Identifying interpretation and translation sources, as well as knowing how to use these resources effectively, is one of the most important duties of a tactical anthropology team in a local community. When conducting a rapid needs assessment within their jurisdiction, the T-CAT should include numerous questions related to the diversity of languages spoken in a community and have a strong sense of language barriers that may exist among some subpopulations. Sources for interpretation and translation should then be identified, advocated for, and supported with budgets in an agency. Some options for interpretation and translation include a) full- or part-time bilingual and bicultural staff or contractors within a public safety organization; b) the purchasing of a subscription to telephone interpretation services by a professional vendor; c) the utilization of tele-interpretation services through off-site interpreters via skype or facetime on tablets, telephones, and laptops, and other electronic devices; d) the identification of trusted and vetted community members from local culturally diverse neighborhoods that can assist with emergency messaging; e) partnering with local universities that may have students that speak foreign languages or ethnic non-profit agencies and associations in the community; and f) pilot test products such as automatic translation apps and websites that can provide a general idea about the content of foreign language material. The tactical anthropology team should recognize that languages fluctuate often in communities, as do the availability of local interpreters, so jurisdictional needs should be monitored regularly. T-CAT members should be fully trained in how to utilize interpreters, as follows:

Tactics, Techniques, and Procedures:

●Speak slowly and carefully when working with interpreters and community members. Repeat key phrases as needed, and use words that are simple.

●Break information down into phrases and short sentences when using an interpreter. Giving that person too much information to interpret verbally will usually lead to missed information and forgotten key points.

●Make sure that the civilians are understanding the information that is being interpreted. If they look confused through their body language, or they are unable to repeat back key bits of information to you, then have the interpreter explain the information again or in a different way.

●Avoid using jargon, idioms, slang, or words that are difficult to understand. Many of these terms do not translate well into other cultures.

•Do not yell or speak more loudly with community members or interpreters just because they may not understand something. The problem is usually related to comprehension of key words, not deafness.

•Speak to the community member, not the interpreter. Many first responders feel more comfortable just talking directly at an interpreter, but that is usually ineffective and rude to the family member requiring the assistance. The focus of the conversation, even if it is in multiple languages, should be between the affected civilians and the responders serving them, not the interpreters.

•Even though you may be using an interpreter, do not be afraid to use emotion in your communication. Even when a member of the public may not understand the information being told to them, they can often read the body language of the first responder. A sense of urgency can still be transmitted from a responder to a family member, even if messaging is going through the filter of an interpreter.

•Maintain appropriate eye contact, body spacing, and other human communication behaviors as appropriate, depending on the culture, age, or gender of the persons being served.

•Screen and vet interpreters carefully! Just because someone speaks a second language does not make them a good interpreter. They must still understand the cultural nuances of the population they are serving, be from the appropriate ethnic group to serve the community, and be completely trusted by them.

•Ensure that interpreters follow ethical procedures, such as not sharing confidential information with others in the community, nor taking payments or tips for help from the population.

•Where possible when resources allow, considering using female interpreters when working with women from more conservative, traditional cultures, as well as older interpreters when working with adults.

•While presenting emergency information, conducting briefings, or the like with large groups of members of the public from different cultural communities, allow audience members to have time to interpret for each other. Check the audience for comprehension of key facts, and clarify as needed.

•When scheduling meetings, briefings, public forums, and other such events with members of the public that do not speak the same language as you do, allow for approximately two-to-three times as long for those encounters, due to interpretation needs.

•Where possible, except in dire emergencies, avoid using family members, especially children, as interpreters and translators. Doing so can be unethical at times, violate confidentiality law, and may disrupt traditional family social order.

•Even though your tactical anthropology team members may be using interpreters for their work in the field, learn a few key phrases in the native language of the community members being served. Saying hello, goodbye, thank you, and "my name is…" can be very helpful, and will make team members seem more approachable, caring, and culturally competent than someone who has not bothered to learn these key phrases in a foreign language.

Drill:

A severe natural disaster has just hit the community where your public safety agency is located. Local fire and emergency medical providers have contacted your tactical anthropology team to ask for interpreters to help with response activities with the public. Develop a rapid plan for your T-CAT to provide interpretation referrals for these agencies, and answer the following questions:

1. What languages are most likely spoken in your jurisdiction?

2. Do you have live interpreters available, or will you recommend the utilization of telephonic or off-site interpreters?

3. What partnering agencies or local resources in your community can you contact to see if they can help with emergency interpretation?

Photo TTP 13: Working with an interpreter to discuss resource needs of Syrian refugees in Turkey.

TTP 14: CONDUCTING T-CAT TRAINING

Overview:

The main objective of this book is to emphasize that cultural knowledge is a tactical skill that can be critically important to effective emergency response and disaster relief operations in public safety agencies. Like any tactical skill, though, it is perishable, and requires ongoing training and education to further develop the set of knowledge and techniques necessary to function effectively in rapidly changing, culturally complex areas of operation. The training necessary to be effective as a tactical cultural asset team can be provided by a variety of sources, including internal departmental instructors, external academies, community colleges, universities, and other sources. Regardless of the source, the training and education for T-CAT members should be ongoing, and include not just learning from manuals, books, and videos, but include practical skill-building sessions as well. Likewise, T-CATs can be invaluable trainers themselves for other public safety professionals in their agencies or jurisdictions on critically important issues related to working effectively in multicultural environments. It is important to note that training on tactical anthropology should generally not take the place of diversity training or other similar programs that may already exist in an organization or jurisdiction. This is a different field, and diversity training typically is extremely limited in the provision of the tactical anthropology skills necessary for responders to understand in helping communities before, during, and after emergencies.

Tactics, Techniques, and Procedures:

•Develop a yearly training schedule for members of the T-CAT. Where resources allow, monthly training meetings are most effective, with ample time to discuss recent missions, requests for services, case reviews, etc.

•Incorporate trainings for the team that include a variety of methods of learning, such as lectures, presentations, video clips, hands-on practice sessions with interviewing, strategic tactical exercises, tabletop practice sessions, and the like.

•When possible, bring in guest speakers from local culturally diverse populations that can share information with the T-CAT regarding best practices in working with these families. Religious leaders, ethnic association representatives, and other key leaders can be excellent presenters and are often willing to speak to public safety representatives.

•Sponsor on-site trainings and meetings. For instance, a T-CAT could hold a monthly meeting in a local community center in a particular refugee neighborhood, and elders from that population could provide field training for the team.

•Develop table top scenarios and strategic field exercises with the organization(s) that the T-CAT serves, so that their skills can be utilized and further developed. For example, a multi-agency search and rescue exercise could create a scenario where a refugee child is missing. The T-CAT would be part of the response team, and could practice family interviewing, conducting cultural briefings for the organization, and other such duties.

•Provide trainings through multiple venues, depending on budget, time, and resources. Trainings can be conducted by the T-CAT or its members through lectures, but can also involve sending a member to an academy or conference to gain specific skills that are later shared with the team. Likewise, local community colleges and/or universities can sometimes send over guest speakers on anthropology topics, or representatives from local cultural communities can conduct briefings as well for the team. Less expensive options would be to view a variety of internet training resources on working cross-culturally, such as short video clips online.

•Utilize the T-CAT as a source of cultural anthropology briefings for the unit it represents. Because T-CATs should maintain a database of information on local communities within the jurisdiction it serves, this can be valuable information to the organization. For instance, the T-CAT could conduct periodic briefings on new local populations in the community; offer guidance on how to work effectively with different groups in the community; provide information on key leaders that want to partner with first responders on emergency issues, and other topics.

Strategic Tactical Exercise:

Utilize the following table to develop a draft schedule of trainings for a tactical cultural asset team in your agency. Also identify ways that your T-CAT could be utilized by agencies in your community to provide briefings and cultural trainings for other first response agencies in your jurisdiction.

SAMPLE TRAINING TOPICS	SOURCE OF TRAINING	LOCATION OF TRAINING	FREQUENCY OF TRAINING
Working with Interpreters			
Conducting Field Interviews			
Identifying and Engaging Key Leaders			
Culturally Specific Trainings (ex: working with Burmese Refugees in the Community)			
Conducting Rapid Needs Assessments			
Working Cross-Culturally with Male and Female Clients			
Understanding Specific Religious Groups in the Community (ex: Orthodox Jews, the Amish, Muslims, etc.)			
Understanding Legal Status Categories			
Working with Elders and Seniors in the Local Community			
Working with Low Literacy Populations			
Working with Low Income Families in Emergencies			
Other Topics			

Photo TTP 14: FEMA long-term recovery training. (Photo by Ruth Kennedy/FEMA photo.)

TTP 15: ASSURING ETHICS IN MISSION OPERATIONS

Overview:

Conducting response operations and programs in the field during emergencies can represent some of the most challenging work in the world for public safety professionals. These difficulties are compounded when the residents involved in a public safety crisis come from dozens of different cultures with unique languages, values, and barriers to effective operations, particularly in settings where the basic infrastructure may be collapsed, the emotions of survivors and responders can be charged, and resources may be severely limited. During these times, particularly if pre-planning has not occurred for such operations, first responders may be tempted to do what needs to be done immediately for the sake of public safety. For instance, emergency messaging may be directed only to the general middle class of a community, with little time or concern for low literacy populations, residents with hearing and vision impairments, and families with language barriers. In other situations, many first reponders feel there is little time to be "politically correct" and "culturally responsive" to every group in an affected area. It is during these challenging times, as well as during the pre-response and recovery phases, that public safety professionals must ensure that their tactical anthropology operations are ethical, transparent, and legal, and do not violate the civil rights of individuals being served.

Tactics, Techniques, and Procedures:

●Be truthful when speaking or meeting with various cultural communities. Transparency in operations is critical to building trust and working with different populations as true partners in response and relief efforts.. If you must break your word, explain why that was done, apologize, take responsibility, and move on.

●Maintain the confidentiality of individuals and families when possible. Many residents and interpreters in cultural communities are related or know each other closely. Information given by a public safety professional to one resident will often be shared quickly with others in many high-context cultures, which can impact operations if privacy needs to be maintained.

●Conduct after action reports and briefings with community members. Invite representatives or leaders from various cultural communities to attend meetings with first responders where possible, so they can provide valuable feedback from the public perspective about the response and relief efforts in their own communities. Listen honestly to their feedback and modify TTPs for future operations as appropriate.

●Provide specialized counseling and training to any first responders on the team that may not have the skills or interest to work cross-culturally in emergencies. If this remedial work is not successful, replace the ineffective team member, as the incompetence of one can affect the reputation of all on the team for years to come in many communities.

•Ensure that those participating in any tactical anthropology operation are genuinely concerned about the well-being of people from all walks of life, capable of providing emergency services fairly, and competent in their interactions with different cultural communities. Not all staff in a public safety agency are qualified to conduct cross-cultural emergency response.

•Avoid stereotyping and profiling, which are generally illegal in most operations. Use legal socio-cultural intelligence instead to better understand general patterns, commonalities, perceptions, and needs within a cultural community as a whole, but do not assume that every single person from that community fits that pattern.

•Recognize "diversity within diversity" and the tremendous cultural differences that are present among all populations in communities. For instance, do not assume that all Hispanics are from Mexico, or that all whites speak English in America. All populations have sub-groups with different backgrounds, beliefs, practices, needs, and attitudes that can sometimes have significant impact on emergency operations.

•Ultimately, ensure that the outcomes in a community are generally equal among the different sub-cultures after a disaster or large-scale emergency. If casualty rates are significantly higher among some groups compared to others, a thorough review must be done to determine the causes and develop special operations to make these rates more equitable with the broader population.

Table Top Exercise:

African American families were disproportionately affected by the mega-storm Hurricane Katrina in New Orleans in 2005 in the United States. Many after action reviews about the disaster indicated that pre-existing social disparities likely played a major role in creating higher casualty rates.

1. Discuss what pre-existing factors might have led to poorer outcomes from this disaster among African Americans from a political, social, economic, and infrastructure disparity perspective.

2. If local public safety agencies had Tactical Cultural Asset Teams, what could those units have done to identify, plan for, and reduce social disparities on a broader level in order to reduce casualties from a disaster?

Photo TTP 15: FEMA outreach in Puerto Rico working with local emergency managers. (Photo by Andrea Booher/FEMA photo.)

SECTION IV:

RESOURCES AND TOOLS

A. Population Change and Human Migration

●International Organization for Migration (IOM). www.iom.int

●United Nations High Commissioner for Refugees. www.unhcr.org

●United Nations Social and Economic Affairs/Population Division. www.un.org/esa/population/

●United States Census Bureau. www.census.gov

●UK Census. Office for National Statistics. https:// www.ons.gov.uk/

●EU Census Hub. Eurostat. http://ec.europa.eu/

●Canada Census of Population. Statistics Canada. http:// www12.statcan.gc.ca/

●Institute for Research into Superdiversity (IRiS). University of Birmingham http://www.birmingham.ac.uk/research/activity/ superdiversity-institute/index.aspx

B. Cultural and Linguistic Diversity

●U.S. Department of Health and Human Services. Cultural and Linguistic Competency for Disaster Preparedness Planning and Crisis Response. https://www.phe.gov/Preparedness/planning/abc/Pages/linguistic.aspx

●The National Resource Center on Advancing Emergency Preparedness for Culturally Diverse Communities. Drexel University. http://www.diversitypreparedness.org/

●Center for Applied Linguistics. Cultural Orientation Resource Center. http://www.cal.org/

●St. Petersburg College. Center for Public Safety Innovation/ National Terrorism Preparedness Institute. https://gp/spcollege.edu/Publicsafety/

C. Honor Violence and Forced Marriage

• The AHA Foundation: Preventing Violence. Ending Shame. Reclaiming Honor. http://www.theahafoundation.org/

• Tahirih Justice Center, Protecting Immigrant Girls and Women against Violence. www.tahirih.org

D. Cultural Knowledge and Skills in Security Settings

●U.S. Army Training and Doctrine Command (TRADOC) Culture Center. http://www.tradoc.army.mil/

●U.S Air Force Culture and Language Center. www.culture.af.mil

●U.S. Marine Corps Center For Advanced Operational Culture And Learning (CAOCL). www.marinecorpsconceptsandprograms.com

●U.S Navy Center for Language, Regional Expertise, and Culture. http://www.netc.navy.mil/centers/ciwt/clrec/

●Defence Centre for Languages and Culture (DCLC). Defense Academy of the United Kingdom. http://www.da.mod.uk/

E. Working Cross-Culturally in "Whole Communities"

- American Ambulance Association. Cross-Cultural Communication for EMS. www.the-aaa.org

- U.S. Federal Emergency Management Administration (FEMA). A Whole Community Approach to Emergency Management: Principles, Themes, and Pathways for Action. www.fema.gov/ja/media-library/assets/documents/23781

- U.S. Department of Homeland Security, Center for Faith-based & Neighborhood Partnerships. www.dhs.gov/dhs-center-faith-based-neighborhood-partnerships

- UK Centre for Crime and Justice Studies. Policing a multicultural society in the 21st century. www.crimeandjustice.org.uk/resources/policing-multicultural-society-21st-century.

- United States Department of Health and Human Services, Substance Abuse and Mental Health Services Administration (SAMHSA), Disaster Training and Technical Assistance (DTAC). http://www.samhsa.gov/dtac

- Drexel University, The National Resource Center on Advancing Emergency Preparedness for Culturally Diverse Communities. http://www.diversitypreparedness.org/

F. Cultural Considerations and Disaster Response

•United Nations Office for Disaster Risk Reduction. http://www.unisdr.org/

•National Center for Disaster Preparedness. Columbia University. http://ncdp.columbia.edu/

•Preventionweb: Serving the Information Needs of the Disaster Risk Reduction Community. http://www.preventionweb.net/english/

•Center for Refugee and Disaster Response. Human Vulnerability to Disasters. Johns Hopkins University. http://www.jhsph.edu/research/centers-and-institutes/center-for-refugee-and-disaster-response/natural_disasters/

•Natural Hazards Center. University of Colorado-Boulder. https://hazards.colorado.edu

•Pacific Disaster Center: Fostering Disaster Resilient Communities. http://www.pdc.org/

•Center for Disaster and Risk Analysis. Colorado State University. http://cdra.colostate.edu/

•Disaster Research Center. University of Delaware. www.drc.udel.edu

G. International Aid Agencies

- United Nations Office for the Coordination of Humanitarian Affairs (OCHA). http://www.unocha.org/

- United Nations Infants, Children and Education Fund (UNICEF). www.unicef.org

- Reliefweb:Informing humanitarians worldwide. Reliefweb.int

- International Federation of Red Cross and Red Crescent Societies. http://www.ifrc.org/

- Oxfam International. www.oxfam.org

- Médecins Sans Frontières/Doctors without Borders.www.msf.org

- Mercy Corps. www.mercycorps.org

- United Nations High Commissioner on Refugees (UNHCR) www.unhcr.org

H. Crisis Communication and Low Literacy

●Cultural and Linguistic Competency in Disaster Preparedness and Response Fact Sheets (RESPOND). United States Department of Health and Human Services. https://www.phe.gov/Preparedness/planning/abc/Pages/linguistic-facts.aspx

●Health Literacy Measurement Tools. Agency for Healthcare Research and Quality. https://www.ahrq.gov/professionals/quality-patient-safety/quality-resources/tools/literacy/index.html

●Health Literacy Tools. Resources and Services Administration. Tools. https://www.hrsa.gov/publichealth/healthliteracy/index.html

●Public Health Emergency Preparedness. Low Literacy Populations and Disaster Communications. U.S. Department of Health and Human Services.https://www.phe.gov/ASPRBlog/Lists/Posts/Post.aspx?ID=190

●Infographics for Disasters. Federal Emergency Management Agency. https://www.fema.gov/media-library/assets/documents/108453

I. Sample T-CAT Task List for Mission Operations

TASK	DONE
Conduct rapid assessment on communities within area of operations	
Review and manage socio-cultural demographic data on populations for planning purposes on an on-going basis (general family structure, average economic level, general literacy levels, estimated size of sub-populations, estimated level of acculturation, etc.)	
Determine primary cultural groups within area of operations (ethnic groups, tribes, clans, or other units as appropriate)	
Determine range of languages spoken and priorities for interpretation	
Identify sources of interpreters and translators	
Identify key community leaders and possible cultural liaisons	
Identify possible community coalition partners (religious organizations, local ethnic associations, anchor employers, neighborhood associations, market owners, etc.	
Conduct key leader engagements and meetings before, during, and after emergencies and disasters	
Determine knowledge level, beliefs, and practices related to emergencies and disaster within key populations, and utilize this information to modify programs as appropriate from first responders	
Determine and provide preferred and alternative modes of emergency messaging and crisis communication with key populations	
Serve as a culturally responsive point of contact for diverse populations seeking more information about the disaster or emergency	
Conduct briefings for first responder agencies or coalitions on cultural context issues in the area of operations, and how to work effectively cross-culturally	
Conduct briefings for cultural communities on disaster and emergency issues	
Other:	

J. Sample Go-Kit Supplies for Tactical Cultural Asset Teams

• Rucksack, duffel bag, or other durable tactical bag

• Waterproof blank notebooks and pens/pencils

• Smart phones, tablets, laptops, or other electronic database tools

• Binder with important community information, including key populations, local languages, contact information for interpreters, contact information for key leaders, important cultural considerations, etc.

• Infographics or other visual translators for disasters and emergencies for lower literacy populations

• Telephones for tele-interpretation or video-interpretation and consultation

• Cultural guidebooks (hard copies or electronic) for key populations

• Official photo identification cards as Tactical Cultural Asset Team Member

• First Responder agency rosters with contact information for key personnel

• Maps of the area of operations

• Small treats for children when working in community field settings where large numbers of children usually gather (gum, pieces of candy, stickers, etc.)

•Disaster and emergency response brochures and other easy-to-understand written material as appropriate in foreign languages as needed

•Additional tactical equipment as needed for specific agencies or missions (flashlights, radios, survival equipment, etc.)

•T-CAT business cards to leave with communities for further information

•T-CAT velcro or embroidered unit identification on go-kit

ABOUT THE AUTHORS

Mark A. Grey, Ph.D. is Professor of Applied Anthropology at the University of Northern Iowa. He is also Adjunct Research Professor with the United States Army War College. Dr. Grey is founder and Director of the UNI New Iowans Center. The New Iowans Center is an award-winning program that provides technical assistance and training to law enforcement agencies, intelligence units, emergency managers and emergency medical personnel dealing with the unique challenges associated with influxes of immigrant and refugee newcomers. He has published extensively in academic and non-academic journals with recent articles in Iowa Law Enforcement Magazine. His books include "New Americans, New Iowans;" "Postville USA: Surviving Diversity in Small-Town America;" and "Health Matters: A Pocket Guide for Working with Diverse Cultures and Underserved Populations." Dr. Grey has won numerous awards for his activities, including the 2013 Friend of Iowa Civil Rights, the Iowan Immigrant Champion Award, One Iowa Award, Iowa Friends of Civil Rights Award, Iowa Council for International Understanding Vision Award, and the Iowa Regents Award for Faculty Excellence. Dr. Grey is an Iowa-licensed Emergency Medical Responder and a nationally certified Search and Rescue Technician. He volunteers for numerous state and local organizations including the American Red Cross, Star One Search and Rescue Team, several FEMA Community Emergency Response Teams (CERT), the Iowa Mortuary Operational Response Team (I-MORT) and the Iowa Attorney General's Human Trafficking Task Force. Dr. Grey serves as a consultant and trainer for the Iowa Departments of Public Safety, Public Health, and Human Services. He is also an instructor for the Iowa Law Enforcement Academy and the Iowa Department of Public Safety Basic Academy. D., Grey is also an active member of International Law Enforcement Educators and Trainers Association.

 **Michele Devlin, Dr.P.H.** is Professor of Global Public Health and Chair of the Division of Health Promotion and Education at the University of Northern Iowa. She is also an Adjunct Research Professor with the United States Army War College. Dr. Devlin is founder of the Iowa Center on Health Disparities there, a model organization established by the National Institutes of Health to improve health equity for underserved populations, and Director of the UNI Global Health Corps humanitarian relief organization. Dr. Devlin completed her doctorate degree in international public health at the University of California at Los Angeles. Her primary areas of specialty include cross-cultural emergency and disaster response with refugee and minority populations, with a particular focus on women and children. She has published nearly 100 articles, reports, papers, and books including "Health Matters: A Guide to Working with Diverse and Underserved Populations" and "Postville USA: Surviving Diversity in Small-Town America." In addition to her academic expertise, Dr. Devlin has more than 25 years of field experience working with public safety, law enforcement, public health, non-profit, and disaster relief organizations around the world that serve in culturally complex communities. Dr. Devlin is the Cultural Awareness Trainer for the Iowa Department of Public Safety and the Iowa Law Enforcement Academies, and a staff trainer for the International Law Enforcement Educators and Trainers Association. She is an international disaster relief team member with the American Red Cross, and has served in Haiti and the Philippines. She has led and/or participated in multiple medical missions around the world in Latin America, Africa, Asia, and the Middle East. Dr. Devlin is a licensed Emergency Medical Responder, and member of the Star One Search and Rescue Team in Iowa; the Iowa Disaster Medical Assistance Team; Disaster Mortuary Operational Team; multiple FEMA Community Emergency Response Teams; and the Medical Reserve Corps. She has provided training and technical assistance on cultural terrain issues to thousands of law enforcement, public safety, search and rescue, disaster response, public health, and emergency management professionals at the federal, state, and local level. Dr. Devlin is the recipient of the One Iowa Award, the Iowa Women's Hall of Fame Award, the Iowa Civil Rights Award, and other local, state, and national honors for outstanding teaching, scholarship, and service. She has extensive travel experience in over 50 nations around the world, and she also served with the U.S. Army Corps of Civilians in Afghanistan during Operation Enduring Freedom as a lead social scientist.

Photo: Sign in Ventura, California thanking fire fighters and first responders during the wildfires of 2017. (Photo by Mark Grey, with permission.)

CPSIA information can be obtained
at www.ICGtesting.com
Printed in the USA
LVHW071725110123
736942LV00010B/402